"*Why Play Works* is an inspiring nity leaders + educators. Jill generously shares a plethora of insights + wisdom + a game plan to maximize the power, value & positive impact that recess can offer. GameON!" #amazing #unlock #cheatcode #gratitude

—Kevin Carroll, author + katalyst

"*WOW. In why play works, Vialet offers a well written, fast moving and compelling case for why play — that seemingly frivolous childhood obsession — holds the seeds to social connectedness, civility and democracy itself. A must read for anyone who cares about children and the future of society and for all who can use a little more recess in their lives.*"

—Kathy Hirsh-Pasek, Professor of Psychology, Temple University; senior fellow Brookings Institution; author Becoming Brilliant and Einstein Never Used Flashcards

"*What this book, celebrating 25 years of Playworks leadership and its proven accomplishments does, is...on close scrutiny, provide a compelling science-based workable narrative and methods for resolving seeming insoluble problems with which our inner city schools (and society) struggle. Problems which historically explode regularly in recess settings that then continue to disrupt the overall school settings, and reflect unsolved broad societal dysfunctions. However, the solutions described in this book work "magically" in many varied and highly challenging settings., But beyond this book are also play based solutions broadly applicable to transforming our polarized society itself. Jill's leadership and Playworks track record and the details within this book provide the keys to providing an antidote to "connection, isolation, fear, distrust and despair, replacing it with joyfulness, resiliency changemaking skills,...and more.*"

—Stuart Brown, MD Founder, National Institute for Play

Why Play Works makes the case for play equity in a moment when we need it more than ever. Vialet has brought together stories, insights and playfulness in a useful, readable format that we hope will shift the thinking of educators, activists and families of the important role of play to physical and mental wellbeing."
—Renata Simril, President and CEO, LA84 & President, Play Equity Fund.

WHY PLAY WORKS

Big Changes Start Small

JILL VIALET

JB JOSSEY-BASS™
A Wiley Brand

Published by John Wiley & Sons, Inc., Hoboken, New Jersey.
Published simultaneously in Canada.

For general information on our other products and services or for technical support, please contact our Customer Care Department within the United States at (800) 762-2974, outside the United States at (317) 572-3993 or fax (317) 572-4002.

Wiley also publishes its books in a variety of electronic formats. Some content that appears in print may not be available in electronic formats. For more information about Wiley products, visit our web site at www.wiley.com.

Library of Congress Cataloging-in-Publication Data

Names: Vialet, Jill, author.
Title: Why play works : big changes start small / Jill Vialet.
Description: [San Francisco] : Jossey-Bass, [2021] | Includes index.
Identifiers: LCCN 2021027139 (print) | LCCN 2021027140 (ebook) | ISBN
  9781119774549 (paperback) | ISBN 9781119779124 (adobe pdf) | ISBN
  9781119775508 (epub)
Subjects: LCSH: Play. | Socialization. | School recess breaks.
Classification: LCC LB1137 .V53 2021 (print) | LCC LB1137 (ebook) | DDC
  306.4/81—dc23
LC record available at https://lccn.loc.gov/2021027139
LC ebook record available at https://lccn.loc.gov/2021027140

Cover image: © Getty Images | Passionartist
Cover design: Paul McCarthy

SKY10028933_080921

Contents

Introduction

In 1995 I was running a small local nonprofit organization called the Museum of Children's Art (mocha) in Oakland, California. We had a number of partnerships with schools—basically artist residencies—and one of them was with a local school named Santa Fe Elementary where Mrs. Peyton was the principal.

Although much of the world has changed since I was a kid, school offices have not. They are typically busy hives of activity, with a counter that keeps visitors from coming in too deep, two desks for the school secretary and another administrative helper, and an inner sanctum—the principal's office—just off to one side. The Santa Fe office was set up just like this, and I recall sitting in one of the chairs generally reserved for students anticipating punishment up against the front wall, waiting for Mrs. Peyton.

The meeting had been scheduled for just after the lunch hour, and Mrs. Peyton was running late. After about 20 minutes, Mrs. Peyton emerged followed by three little boys. The young men seemed about nine or ten years old, and they all looked absolutely miserable. Mrs. Peyton, in turn, was furious. She ushered the boys to the school secretary, conveyed some instructions about contacting their families and then marched back into her office, stopping briefly to signal that I should follow.

Once in the office, I sat in the chair opposite hers and, before I had fully settled in, Mrs. Peyton launched into the litany of reasons that, basically, recess was hell. The teachers found every reason to be anywhere but the playground, the students didn't know how to get a game going or to keep a game going, the conflicts that arose on the playground followed the students back into the classroom, and, most frustratingly, these same three boys kept getting into trouble. She was building up steam as she went, and the description of the scene that she painted sounded hopeless. But the thing I remember most clearly was when she said, "And the worst part is that, because of recess, these boys are starting to believe that they're bad kids. These are not bad kids."

I hadn't said anything yet, but I must have nodded or signaled some sort of understanding because Mrs. Peyton took a breath and asked, *"Can't you do something? Can you help fix recess?"*

Initially, I was taken aback by the question. After all, I was there in her office to talk about the artist residency program. But the question got me thinking, and I immediately flashed on my own childhood growing up in Washington, DC, and afternoons spent at the Macomb Street playground. There was a guy who worked for the DC Parks and Rec Department named Clarence who was responsible for all the assorted activities that happened at the park. Mostly I remember him keeping the center open and coaching various teams—basketball and flag football most distinctly. There was the occasional DC Metro spelling bee that some of the kids participated in, and I think there must have been arts and crafts, but generally speaking we just hung out until it was time to go home for dinner.

It's not insignificant that I so vividly recall the basketball and football. This was the 1970s and Title IX had passed in 1972, so although there was a growing shift in attitudes about making opportunities available to women and girls, from my young perspective, it largely meant that I got to play with the boys.

When Mrs. Peyton asked if I might "do something," my immediate thought was how Clarence had always made sure that I got in the game. I was a good athlete and although Clarence didn't make it a big deal, I had a vague sense that he had preemptively squashed any resistance that might have arisen to my participation as a girl. And so, when Mrs. Peyton asked, "Can't you do something? Can you help fix recess?" the first thing I thought was: I could make it possible for every kid to have a Clarence.

That was 25 years ago. Since then I've learned a lot about how to make it possible for kids "to have a Clarence." I've also learned a lot about the power of play, especially when someone like Clarence is making it accessible. The organization I founded back in 1996, originally called Sports4Kids and now called Playworks, works through direct service and more indirectly through training and online support. Our original model, which we now refer to as Coach, involves a full-time staffperson (the Clarence) placed at an elementary school and overseeing four main components: Recess, Class Gametime, the Junior Coach Leadership Program, and Leagues. We'll go a little more into each of these, but here's a little context.

Recess

This is why schools typically ask for Playworks' help. Our staff person is out at all the recesses being the grown-up "in charge."

Class Gametime

At schools where timing allows, our coaches makes themselves available to support classroom teachers running games and physical activities either out on the playground or in the classroom. These smaller groups allow for students to learn the rules to new games, reinforce behavioral norms, and enjoy additional minutes of physical activity. In some cases, the classroom teachers and the coach are able to coordinate ways that Classroom Gametime reinforces classroom lessons, such as a collective running activity tied to mapping distances.

Junior Coach Leadership Program

This is our effort to ensure that kids really own recess. Ten to 12 students—usually fourth and fifth graders—are identified to work in teams supporting the flow of activities out at recess. This includes everything from distributing equipment to introducing new games, from providing oversight at different game stations to helping resolve conflicts when they arise. One thing about this program worth mentioning is that we make a concerted effort to ensure that it doesn't fall into the trap of just involving the "usual" leadership suspects. As you will see, part of the program's success has always stemmed from the diversity of its participants.

The Leagues

The Playworks sports leagues were initially launched to prompt greater involvement among girls, but it has evolved over the years to include an assortment of sports available for all students. We also expanded the offerings to include ongoing leagues in the traditional sense, along with weekend extravaganzas that allowed for short-term competitions. The leagues are also the primary way we involve families and intentionally introduce competition into our programming.

* * *

The results of these efforts when taken together are really quite extraordinary. A randomized control trial—the gold standard of evaluations in which schools were randomized to receive Playworks and the outcomes were measured against comparable schools not engaged with us—found that students at Playworks schools felt safer (according to their teachers), engaged in more vigorous physical activity, were less likely to engage in bullying behaviors, and recovered instructional time with quicker, less fraught transitions.[1] Outcomes, it should be noted, that feel particularly relevant to this moment.

Playworks has weathered many storms since its inception, but recent events have left many of us reeling. As of this writing, kids, families and schools across the US are facing incredible challenges: a global pandemic that has closed many of our schools and a social reckoning that has exposed the institutional racism that our country is built on. In summer 2020, in response to school closings, I worked with staff to write *The Playworks School Re-Opening Workbook*, which we made available as a free ebook.[2] Summer 2020 was also a time of tremendous racial upheaval in the United States, sparked by the murders of George Floyd and others. On the surface, the *Re-Opening Workbook* was an effort to offer some tools and a framework for educators to think about how they wanted to come back; however, the writing of it raised a deeper question. Specifically, what might play teach us about doing things differently *after* schools reopen?

Although play may be the furthest things from our minds when our children's basic education feels threatened, I'm here to say that it is essential for growing kids who are kind and compassionate, able to solve problems, and community oriented. Prioritizing play is critical because these are the very attributes we need for turning things around now and navigating our increasingly complex world.

Play is uniquely well suited to encourage and support human connection. Play has, in fact, survived evolution despite being a "risky" behavior, precisely because it teaches us how to navigate the kind of social connection that is needed right now.

Play also creates many opportunities for redesigning what we want our schools to look like. Considering this moment as a global transition, play offers tremendous lessons for promoting inclusion and belonging. It also makes plain the importance of agency, trust, and their connection to the processes of establishing rules, rituals, and ways of gracefully resolving disagreements. Play teaches us that *it matters how it feels*, and that focusing on that in school reopenings—for everyone involved—will be critical to our ultimate success.

Writing the *Re-Opening Workbook* also reminded me of all the many different people who have been part of the Playworks story. So, in writing this book, I reached out to lots and lots of people: folks who had worked at Sports4Kids in the early days, as well as people who had joined when we had already made the shift to calling ourselves Playworks. I talked with principals who had had our program, to researchers who had studied our program, and to funders who had supported our program. My hope was that in talking to the people who knew us best, I could come to better understand why play works.

This book is the result. The stories and lessons learned from 25 years of bringing play to schools all across the country (and in Ireland as you will read) provide the backbone of this effort to share one profound insight: *play has the power to bring out the best in people*. This book is not intended to be a history of Playworks, but rather a collection of insights about play that I hope will be inspiring and helpful for anyone who has power or influence over children's access to safe and healthy daily play. My hope is that in reading this book you will come to understand why prioritizing play is so important, not only to the individual child but also to our collective well-being.

Why Play Works looks at play through our experience as an organization and through our observations as facilitators of play. This book also asks us to reconsider how we have been doing things, and how we might do these things better. The future is uncertain. This book is an effort to inspire and support a shift in our educational system to focus more deeply on teaching the skills that are essential to thriving in a democracy—the abilities to navigate social connection, to have respectful conflict, to learn from mistakes, and to win graciously. It is also a declaration that play is critical to achieving this seismic shift and that big changes start small.

How to Use this Book

I imagine that if you're reading this book, it's because you already have an intuition that play is far more influential than we usually acknowledge. Maybe you've had a striking play experience with your own kids—or your students or the young athletes you coach—and now you're trying to make sense of it. Maybe you're hoping to figure out how you might intentionally tap the power of play—or to convince other grown-ups of what you've discovered. In any and all of these situations, *Why Play Works* is for you.

Why Play Works is organized into three main sections. It starts out with a brief exploration of the theory and the science behind the power of play and the surprisingly challenging task of actually defining *play*. I can imagine that some of you might be tempted to skip over this seemingly academic opening, but I'd encourage you to at least skim it. This section is really the foundation of understanding *why* you should care about play and provides some persuasive ideas for anyone who is trying to convince others of play's importance.

The second section, and really the heart of the book, is made up of **Twenty Big Changes** where play can offer a powerful small start. The book digs into the role of play in creating social norms, promoting social connection and physical activity, along with the relationship among play, safety, risk, and learning. The Playworks experience provides a great springboard for exploring play and leadership (primarily through the lens of our Junior Coach Leadership Program), and lessons learned from running sports leagues offer a chance to consider the issues of gender, competition, and the role of families. Throughout the book I've tried to illustrate how play can serve as a powerful lever of design in creating intentional teaching and learning moments. I also look at how play can work in conjunction with space and place, including the regional differences we've encountered bringing Playworks to new cities across the US, in expanding our efforts to Ireland, and most recently translating our approach to work virtually. Finally, I've included thoughts on the change that is possible through the connection between race and play, and the role of play in healing.

Each of the **Twenty Big Changes** has an accompanying **Power of Play**—insights related to how these changes show up at school—and a **Small Start**—a game or activity that is intended to make concrete the way that play can serve as a catalyst. I've also included a bunch of my favorite game recipes at the end of the book, and you can share those with others by sending them to the link: www.playworks.org/whyplayworksgameguide.

You'll also find a few **Time-Outs** mixed in—ideas that offer slightly different ways of thinking about play, intended to spark your curiosity about the changes you might achieve.

The third and final section of *Why Play Works*, **We Can Do This**, looks at the role of adults in promoting play. This section is my call to action—an invitation to the reader to consider how you might become a more active enabler of play and the big changes it can prompt.

* * *

This is a critical moment in the American experiment. The polarization that defines our public discourse is extreme, and there is a pervasive sense of hopelessness about the possibility of finding common ground. This book sets out to show how play is precisely the counterintuitive solution we need at this moment. Although frequently dismissed as frivolous, nothing could be further from the truth. Play is the antidote to disconnection, isolation, fear, distrust, and despair. It can help in mitigating trauma while building the confidence and resilience essential to navigating risk. It is a source of joy that facilitates understanding across difference. It taps our intrinsic motivation, teaches us to deal with the unexpected, and sparks creativity. Play is where we learn the changemaking skills—the everyday, inclusive leadership skills—that this moment so desperately requires. With this book, I invite you to suspend your disbelief and to consider how play might work for you, your community, and our democracy.

Notes

1   Bleeker, M., S. James-Burdumy, N. Beyler, A. H. Dodd, R. A. London, L. Westrich, K. Stokes-Guinan, and S. Castrechini. "Findings from a Randomized Experiment of Playworks" (April 17, 2012). Mathematica Policy Research and the John W. Gardner Center for Youth and Their Communities.

2   www.playworks.org/workbook.

Play, Seriously:
The Theory
and Science Behind Play

You may be wondering why I'm starting out with this overview of the foundational, big ideas behind play. The truth is that I wasn't all that familiar with any of these theories or the science of play when I launched Sports4Kids—nor when we changed the name to Playworks. It would have helped. It would have made it easier to convince some people and to explain away other people's reservations. I'm not sure it would have radically changed any of our choices, but it might have informed them. And knowledge is power.

All that said, as you will see, a key element of play is volition. My hope is that your engagement with this book will be as playful as possible, and so, by all means, skip ahead to the next section if you so choose. But know that you are cordially invited to spend a little time here learning about play's storied history—*play* defined, play theory, and the emerging field of play science.

What's in a Name?

It's true that a better understanding of the ideas behind play might have influenced our name change. For the first 13 years we were known as Sports4Kids. This name had seen us from almost the very beginning (we were briefly Kidsports until receiving a cease and desist order from another organization). It had accompanied us through significant growth in staff—including opening new offices in cities across the country, the development of our leagues, and our first big AmeriCorps grant. It was the name we were using when the Robert Wood Johnson Foundation (RWJF) decided to invest an astronomical $4.4 million in an initial plan to achieve national scale. And, perhaps most importantly, Sports4Kids was the name—with its accompanying logo—that was on literally thousands of t-shirts that staff and students wore with a sense of pride and belonging.

Changing an organization's name is a surprisingly complicated undertaking. Not so much in the actual logistics of it—those are fairly straightforward. The complicated part comes in managing all the emotions associated with a name change. To our credit, we didn't take the emotional aspect of our name change lightly. The entire process took almost 18 months from the initial idea of looking at redesigning our logo through deciding to do a whole rebrand, to selecting the name and actually producing new t-shirts. Looking back, it seems clear that one of the most important aspects of this shift was in developing our ability to explain why. Why Playworks? It was so important—especially for our staff—that the story wasn't simply why *not* Sports4Kids, even if the 4 in the middle did seem hopelessly 1980s in the rearview mirror. Our name change had to be about becoming something bigger.

With support from RWJF, we worked with a friend and board member, Dru DeSantis, and her firm DeSantis Breindel to go through a very professional process. The team interviewed stakeholders—students, principals, staff, and funders—about the nature of our programming and impact. They generated concepts, solicited suggestions, and made presentations. They brought in two industry superstars—women from Miami, referred to somewhat mysteriously as "the naming ladies," who generated a list of over 500 names that I remember spending hours poring over.

There was a lot of creativity and a few false starts. We briefly fell in love with the name "Big Bounce," until someone pointed out that our female staff members might not be super-psyched to have that emblazoned on their chests. There was another name—that now escapes me—that I knew we absolutely had to have, but someone else owned it.

Playworks wasn't actually on the list. It emerged during a presentation to staff members when we were stalled and decided to go back to the drawing board and review what we knew. Dru was walking us through a slide deck—yet again—on all our various attributes and values, emphasizing what principals and teachers said about our impact over and over again. In summation she noted, "Play works." Our then executive director David Rothenberg and then COO Elizabeth Cushing looked at each other, and we had found our new name.

Defining *Play*

But why the shift from sports to play? Sports hold a funny place in American life. Although many people in the US *love* sports, there is a not-insignificant population that see sports as somewhat suspect. Some of these humans work in schools, and they would argue that they have been driven to this position by the extreme way we push young people into sports. They see sports as competition for the time and attention of their students and a distraction from the "real" work of teaching and learning.

Play and sports, although deeply connected, aren't exactly the same. Usually in sports your goal is trying to win. And that really does change everything. One of my favorite definitions of a game comes from the philosopher Bernard Suits, who explains a game as the "voluntary attempt to overcome unnecessary obstacles."[1] Fundamentally, there is an attitudinal difference between having an end goal or not. It's not that play isn't serious and sports are—play can be extraordinarily serious. It's not that play is always fun, either. People often think of play as the opposite of work, but as the New Zealand play theorist Brian Sutton-Smith wrote, "The opposite of play is not work. The opposite of play is depression."[2] The difference is really in the fundamental question, "to what end?"

Defining *play* is a tricky thing to do. It's a little like the old saying about pornography, "you know it when you see it." Play theorists have debated the definition for as long as there have been play theorists. In his 1955 book *Homo Ludens,* Johan Huizinga defined *play* as "a free activity standing quite consciously outside 'ordinary' life . . . 'not serious,' but at the same time absorbing the player intensely and utterly."[3] Developmental psychologist Lev Vygotsky limited his discussion of play to the make-believe play of preschoolers, and Maria Montessori maintained that play was the work of a child, emphasizing the importance of play based in reality.[4]

Mildred Parten proposed a system of classification for play in the 1930s that is still commonly used in child development. Her system was originally made up of six categories: unoccupied play, onlooker behavior, solitary independent play, parallel play, associative play, and cooperative play. Subsequent sociologists have added five additional categories: dramatic/fantasy play, competitive play, symbolic play, physical play, and constructive play.[5]

More recently, Dr. Stuart Brown's book, *Play: How It Shapes the Brain, Opens the Imagination, and Invigorates the Soul*, takes a stab at defining the activity, laying out the essence of play in seven properties: purposeless, voluntary, inherent attraction, freedom from time, diminished consciousness of self, improvisational potential, and continuation desire.[6] Like everything else in play theory, these seven properties have been debated extensively. Is play marked by purposelessness or the absence of *apparent* purpose? Can you be forced to play? If you are extrinsically motivated, does that diminish the value of play? What about when play stops being fun?

The one thing that all the play theorists seem to agree on is the importance of play being voluntary. This emphasis on choice also feels like the characteristic that has the greatest influence on the experience of play in schools, providing students with a direct understanding of the difference between engagement and compliance. As a result, play can be a source of uneasiness for adults who see their job as maintaining control, even as it offers a powerful springboard for encouraging students to be the drivers of their own education.

In an interview with the *American Journal of Play,* Dr. Brown offered a wonderful definition: "Play is an ancient, voluntary, inherently pleasurable, apparently purposeless activity or process that is undertaken for its own sake and that strengthens our muscles and our social skills, fertilizes brain activity, tempers and deepens our emotions, takes us out of time, and enables a state of balance and poise."[7] He goes on to emphasize the importance of play being voluntary, suggesting that when an activity becomes compulsive—or an addiction—it can no longer be play because you are no longer really choosing it. "When play ceases to be voluntary, it ceases to be play."

A Brief Tour of Play Theory

In the early 1900s, play theorists proposed the idea that children build up an excess of energy and that active play is required to work off that surplus. And although play theory has come to recognize a far greater complexity, this understanding is still very commonly held, especially in schools. Initially suggested by Friedrich von Schiller in the 18th century and expanded on by the psychologist Herbert Spencer in 1873, the idea is that our evolution from hunter-gatherers has left us with excess energy that makes prolonged sitting a challenge.

For children's play, at least, Anthony Pellegrini and John Evans refuted this understanding in a 1997 article entitled "Surplus Energy Theory: An Enduring but Inadequate Justification for school Break-Time."[8] Evans and Pellegrini note that the argument is physiologically unsound and points to children's willingness to play beyond exhaustion—after their "surplus energy" is spent—as well as children's willingness to opt to stay inside when given the choice of quiet sedentary activities—hinting toward a lack of "surplus energy"—as evidence. Further, as I have frequently witnessed in schools prior to Playworks programming, it is not uncommon for only a few children to engage in "moderate to vigorous" physical activity during free play. Clearly not all kids are bursting to release some energy.

Pellegrini and Evans argue that the root of children's restlessness in class after extended periods of sitting reflects not the surplus energy theory but the novelty theory. The novelty theory suggests that students become bored with the activities they are engaged with and become inattentive in anticipation of doing something different, such as getting to go outside. Playing represents the opportunity to do something new—something potentially self-defined, active, and spontaneous. Pellegrini and Evans conclude the article with an emphatic endorsement of the importance of play, arguing that it is essential that we see play as more than just a break from work to prepare for more work. What is lost in reducing play to simply a way of releasing energy is the understanding of play as an opportunity for children to use their creativity while developing their imagination, dexterity, and physical, cognitive, and emotional strength.

Perhaps the biggest developments in play theory happened in the 1960s, when Swiss psychologist Jean Piaget looked at the connection between children's play and their stages of development, bucketing play into four different types: functional, constructive, symbolic/fantasy, and games with rules.[9] Piaget and his followers were somewhat dismissive of the final category, games with rules because of their reliance on someone to be an arbitrator of the rules (often a grown-up), and symbolic/fantasy play was held up as its highest form. Because every area of study needs conflict and drama, there was, and continues to be, debate about this. The aforementioned play theorist Brian Sutton-Smith offered a critique of Piaget's theory and later wrote a book called *The Ambiguity of Play,* looking not only at the definition of play, but also at the "rhetoric" of play—essentially the ideologies that have been used to prioritize some forms of play over others.[10]

Time-Out: Structured Versus Unstructured Play

The debate about the value of play—and more specifically the difference between play with rules and other forms of play—continues to this day, largely characterized as structured versus free play. Over the years, Playworks has been criticized for what was perceived as our emphasis on structured play. Although the free-play folks haven't always been huge fans of Playworks, we generally feel quite warmly about free play. Peter Gray is a psychologist and professor at Boston College who has written extensively on the importance of "freedom to learn," basically the idea that kids come into the world curious to learn and that this instinct drives them to play.[11] The job of grown-ups, in this framing, is to create environments that support children's innate curiosity and, as much as possible, to stay out of the way.

Professor Gray was originally introduced to Playworks by a reporter who was writing about our approach and looking for someone to offer a more critical, and ideally negative, analysis. When Playworks was described as a program that brought in recess coaches to coordinate student play at the break time, Peter was initially willing. It sounded, given the way that the reporter described it, like the ultimate infringement on students having choice and voice during the time in the school day that is often the last bastion of student control. When he actually learned more about our work with a visit to see our program in action at a school in Boston, however, it dramatically changed his understanding.

> My view of Playworks was shaped by two observations. First, is the horrible observation that the recess length was only 15 minutes. This is a crime. It is not enough time for children to play. Given that, it seemed beneficial to have a young adult help get something started. I noticed that there was no requirement to participate and that the young Playworks person did a good job of stepping out and letting the kids take control once the game was started. I also learned from a friend (who was a math consultant visiting many schools in Boston) that the Playworks facilitator was typically the most popular person at school and was bringing a more playful attitude to everyone.

Watching Playworks coaches connect with students by creating a structure for play that the students could successfully navigate and ultimately control, emphasizing student volition, and ultimately protecting the time against school concerns about issues of safety, Peter came to see our work—although not his first choice—as nonetheless a necessary defense of play in schools.

UC Santa Cruz sociologist Rebecca London has spent much of the past 10 years studying recess, with a particular focus on Playworks. In her book, *Rethinking Recess: Creating Safe and Inclusive Playtime for All Children in School,* she offers that Playworks' approach falls outside this debate by providing an alternative: organized play.

> Recess, like any other time of the school day, requires some planning. My research findings demonstrate that schools can create a positive recess environment through planning and organization that is neither structured nor unstructured and that supports both physical activity and social and emotional growth. It is not a simple one-size-fits-all approach, but rather a customized approach to recess planning and organization that requires firsthand knowledge of the school context and the students' needs—information that all school administrators already have. Given the potential benefits and drawbacks of both structured and unstructured recess approaches, and the multiple ways that schools can support students to develop, this hybrid approach of organized recess makes the most sense and has been proven to be effective.[12]

Play Science

Most mammals begin life—and their exploration of the world—through play. Stuart Brown looks closely at the connection between animal behavior and play in his work, with a particular focus on the detrimental impact of play deprivation. Brown compares the science of play to the science of sleep and argues compellingly that its implications for neuroscience are comparable. Thinking about sleep, and how our understanding of its importance has changed dramatically over time, is a useful point of comparison. As Dr. Brown has pointed out, back in the 1940s, sleep was just as "undefined and enigmatic" as play is today.

Rats are often cited as the optimal animal to study in exploring the neurobiology of play because they are exceptionally playful prior to rat puberty, displaying play behaviors before they are even weaned. Although rats that are systematically bred for certain physiological and/or behavioral traits demonstrate differing degrees of playfulness, postnatal experiences have been shown to significantly influence rat play as well. The amount of licking and grooming rats received has been correlated to less fearful rat pups, and although extended separation from the mother rat has negative impact on pup behavior, consistent and brief daily separations from the mother rat are linked to increased play behavior. Interestingly, these brief separations are also connected to an increase in licking and grooming by the mother rat, creating a self-reinforcing system.

Although there is still much to be learned about the neuroscience behind human play, it has been the subject of research for over half a century, building on the foundation of understanding of animal behaviors. Dr. Joe Frost wrote at length on the subject beginning in the 1970s, and more recently Dr. Jane McGonigal has written and spoken extensively about the neuroscience behind video games. More research is needed to better understand the connections between play and neural activity. What is clear is that playful learning experiences that are characterized by joy, meaning, active engagement, repetition, and social connection are associated with increased dopamine levels, stimulating networks in the brain associated with memory, metacognition, analogical thinking, creating insight, motivation, and reward.[13]

The science about mirror neurons reinforces the idea of play benefiting our brains, even as the popular beliefs about mirror neurons may have gotten out a bit ahead of what the science has fully determined. Much of what is known is based largely on research involving adult monkeys, where mirror neurons have been documented firing both when an animal acts and when the animal observes the same action performed by another. Thus, the neuron "mirrors" the behavior of the other, as though the observer were itself acting. Some researchers believe this explains how we learn to generate our own actions and how we monitor and interpret the actions of others, and other researchers maintain that it could point to the neural basis of empathy. This connects to play because shared joy unites us, supporting attunement and a sense of understanding that enable us to collaboratively adapt to complex situations. Looked at from this perspective, play's impact on the brain is essential not just to our survival but also to our potential to collectively thrive.

Finally, Alison Gopnik, author of *The Scientist in the Crib,* has been a strong advocate for considering how early human development might influence models of machine intelligence, with an emphasis on curiosity as a critical part of the process.[14] In her more recent book, *The Gardener and the Carpenter,* Gopnik unpacks the role of parents and caregivers in supporting this curiosity and the importance of creating the conditions that encourage children's brains to do the deeply complex work of creating causal models. As we will explore deeper in this book, among the most important of these conditions is the opportunity to play and make discoveries that are free from expectations, filled with magic, and disconnected from any apparent purpose.

* * *

Phew that was a lot! For those of you who appreciate the age-old teaching strategy of "review and summarize," here you go:

Play **is tricky to define to everyone's satisfaction,** in part because we all have a personal experience of some kind and in part because it is expressed and offers value in so many different ways. (Plus some of us have really strong feelings about it!) One way to understand play is to observe and consider all the ways play shows up in your own life, as well as all the ways we use the words *play* and *playing* and *player* in our day-to-day lives. It's also important to connect the ubiquitous presence of play with the different feelings we get from it. And that's what the rest of this book is about.

One critical aspect of play is volition; individuals get to choose what and how they play. Volition is not equivalent to lack of rules or structures. It's simply a recognition that we want to choose when to jump in and play with each other. We don't want to be forced or compelled. And in our experience, creating the conditions for children to be inspired to play is a powerful lever to achieve all the benefits play offers (see next bullet).

Scientific research has identified a wide array of benefits and developmental impacts from play, some obvious like physical activity and others not so obvious, such as "fertilizing brain activity." Play is one of those subjects about which science has a lot more to learn. How fun!

The debate between the relative value of structured and unstructured play might be getting in our way, if what we care about is making more play happen. And now you have to read the rest of the book to really understand more about that.

Let's play on!

Notes

1 Suits, Bernard. *The Grasshopper: Games, Life and Utopia*. Broadview Press, 2005 (first published 1978), 41.

2 Sutton-Smith, Brian. *The Ambiguity of Play*. Harvard University Press, 2001, 198.

3 Huizinga, Johan. *Homo Ludens*. Random House, 1938, 13.

4 Montessori, Maria. *Child's Instinct to Work*. AMI Communications, 1973.

5 Parten, Mildred B. "Social Participation among Pre-School Children." *The Journal of Abnormal and Social Psychology* 27 (1932): 243–269.

6 Brown, Stuart. *Play: How It Shapes the Brain, Opens the Imagination, and Invigorates the Soul*. Penguin Group, 2009.

7 "Discovering the Importance of Play through Personal Histories and Brain Images An Interview with Stuart L. Brown." *American Journal of Play* 1, 4 (2009): 399–412.

8 Evans, John, and Anthony Pellegrini. "Surplus Energy Theory: An Enduring but Inadequate Justification for School Break-Time." *Educational Review* 49, 3 (1997): 229–236.

9 McLeod, S. A. "Jean Piaget's Theory of Cognitive Development: Background and Key Concepts of Piaget's Theory." *Simply Psychology* (June 6, 2018).

10 Sutton-Smith, Brian. *The Ambiguity of Play*. Harvard University Press, 2001.

11 Gray, P. *Free to Learn: Why Unleashing the Instinct to Play Will Make Our Children Happier, More Self-Reliant, and Better Students for Life*. Basic Books/Hachette Book Group, 2013.

12 London, Rebecca. *Rethinking Recess: Creating Safe and Inclusive Playtime for All Children in School*. Harvard Education Press, 2019, 66.

13 Claire Liu, S. Lynneth Solis, Hanne Jensen, Emily Hopkins, Dave Neale, Jennifer Zosh, Kathy Hirsh-Pasek, and David Whitebread. *Neuroscience and Learning through Play: A Review of the Evidence*. The Lego Foundation, November 2017.

14 Alison Gopnik, "AIs Versus Four-Year-Olds: Looking at What Children Do May Give Programmers Useful Hints About Directions for Computer Learning," in John Brockman (ed.), *Possible Minds*. Penguin, 2019.

Twenty Big
Changes
That Start with Play

Relationships, Relationships, Relationships

Playworks' vice president, Michelle Serrano, started out with us back in 2006 as a coach in East San Jose. That first year, a fourth grader named Jose showed up at Michelle's school, Mildred Goss Elementary, arriving from Mexico in the middle of January. Michelle has a vivid memory of her principal, Mr. Schmaedick, personally bringing Jose out to meet her on the playground. Jose spoke very little English and Michelle spoke little Spanish, but the moment Jose saw other kids playing soccer on the playground, his face lit up. And when one of Michelle's junior coaches—without provocation—called out for him to join the game, everything changed for Jose. Michelle described Jose's transformation from outsider to insider as palpable and immediate. She also recalled Mr. Schmaedick looking relieved and proud. They had worked hard to set the expectations among students that they would welcome new friends and that belonging was a core value for the Goss Gators.

Power of
Play:

One of the most important things the extended youth development community agrees on is that caring adult relationships significantly contribute to young people's well-being—academic, behavioral, and psychological. Although a web of these relationships is ideal, research suggests that even just one consistent relationship with a caring adult has a dramatic impact. In their book *Who You Know: Unlocking Innovations That Expand Students' Networks*, authors Julia Freeland Fisher and Daniel Fisher conclude, "Nothing has more impact in the life of a child than positive relationships."[1]

It's worth taking a moment to consider who that adult was for you: A teacher? A coach? A parent? A cousin? There are people who significantly influence our life trajectory, and understanding how this happened for ourselves is a great place from which to start in imagining how we might have that kind of influence in the lives of others.

Adults have the potential to play many different roles in our children's lives. They may be teachers, mentors, coaches, cheerleaders, as well as sources of accountability and standard bearers for community expectations. The degree to which adults are able to positively fulfill any of these responsibilities is in direct proportion to their ability to relate. Building an authentic relationship that is consistent and caring between an adult and child requires breaking down the inherent power dynamic.

That sounds so serious and yet it is easy to do by playing together. Consider these aspects of play and how they connect to building relationships:

- Play is low stakes. Kids and adults alike can enter a game of Four Square knowing that it is just a game; we're playing for no purpose other than to have fun. We can relax in that environment and let go of what the grown-ups might otherwise want the children to accomplish, changing the dynamic of the relationship.
- We can broaden our roles by playing. We can let go of the official roles we play in the world and just be participants in a game of Wall Ball. That experience is shared and our sameness as players blurs the lines of our differences in age and experience.
- Play is the original amateur activity. Very few of us are world champions at Band Aid Tag, whether we are 6 or 60 years old. That means we are able to share an experience in a similar way, not as experts trying to impart our knowledge from one to the other.
- Kids know they have mastery at play. Creating room for a child to be great at something, like hopping to the finish line while the adult struggles more, gives that child a chance to see that adult in a new light. If the adult is willing to look silly doing something, the child might imagine being able to trust them in more serious moments.

People rely on community to make sense of the world around them. For better and worse, we incorporate the responses of others in modulating our own responses, and we internalize the feelings and reactions of others in determining our own attitudes. The dramatic events of 2020 and the ensuing limitations on direct human contact have made the importance of school and work-place culture more evident than ever. In the absence of direct contact, we fill this vacuum with virtual connection, and in the current age of social media, that means amplifying echo chambers.

The impacts of COVID-19 have not been experienced equally. For some students it has resulted in serious academic losses; other students—typically those from more resourced families—have managed to stay on track. Similarly, some students have experienced the pandemic as a period of profound play deprivation, and others have had more access to unsupervised play than ever before. Although the impact of the traumas experienced from the loss of loved ones and heightened economic and food insecurity will inevitably be significant as schools reopen and into the future—for students and staff—it is hard to anticipate how the social impacts of isolation and lost opportunities for play and social connection will manifest.

We find
Connection
through Play

Play is how we learn to navigate the complexities of social connection. By enabling us to build the foundations of trust and empathy, the experience of play is one of the best ways to learn the skills of being an engaged participant in a democracy—a changemaker who has the confidence to take action when she sees something that she can do to make the world a better place, who has the capacity to collaborate with others that enables success, and who has the confidence that her voice will be heard. These experiences also contribute to the resilience needed to handle the challenges of disconnection.

Developing positive relationships requires strong social skills, and strong social skills require the opportunity to practice and make mistakes and learn. Play is an essential opportunity for students to master the competencies of social emotional learning: self-awareness, social awareness, relationship skills, and responsible decision-making. Developing this set of skills is how we learn to navigate social connections.

Social connection shows up most visibly in schools in the sense of community—how do the students, staff, and families interact inside and beyond the classroom? One of the things that often surprises people is how the experiences on the playground have such an outsized impact on the larger school climate. When things are going poorly out at recess, it follows the students back into the classroom—and into the hallways and the library and the cafeteria and onto the school bus. But when things are going well—when students feel like they get to choose what they are going to play, that they have the tools and permission to resolve their own conflicts, that they understand the rules and feel confident that their peers will also follow them, and that, if not, there is a caring and consistent adult who will help set things right—that collective goodness spills over into the entire school day.

Small
Start:

Building community requires that we get to know one another, and play is one of the most effective ways to make that happen. To this end, the game **I Love My Neighbor** (known as Move Your Butt when played with older youth and Stand Up when played with adults in an auditorium) is a great way to help a group of people quickly and easily get to know one another. When playing with younger students you need a cone for all but one of the participants, arranged in a big circle so that players standing and touching their cone with their foot can see everyone else. The one participant without a cone stands in the middle and he or she completes the statement "I love my neighbor who _____" with something that is true about themselves, such as "I love my neighbor who has a dog." All players for whom this statement is true have to leave their cone in search of a new cone—the cone immediately next to you is not an option—and whoever ends up without a cone is now in the middle and makes the next "I love my neighbor" statement.

If there is a tie when reaching a new cone, students use Rock-Paper-Scissors (we call it RoShamBo and I explain the rules in Big Change 3 on the off chance that you don't know them) to determine who stays at the cone. For older students you can change the sentence from "I love my neighbor. . . ." to "Move your butt if. . . ." And for grown-ups in an auditorium, I often invite the audience to get to know each other a little bit—and to be reminded of what it feels like, even fleetingly, to play—by modifying the game to Stand Up. As in, "Stand Up if you have any Justin Timberlake music on you iPod or MP3 player. . . ."

Testing,
Testing 1, 2, 3

When Coach Kaitlyn arrived at her school just outside Boston, a number of the other staff members gave her a heads-up that there was one fourth-grade student in particular, Adonis, who could be challenging. Kaitlyn made a mental note, but Adonis didn't really participate in any of the activities that she was coordinating until later that spring when he asked to join the volleyball team. Kaitlyn agreed and, indeed, when Adonis first started coming to practices he proved to be a bit disruptive. Over the course of the season as Kaitlyn encouraged his positive behaviors and discouraged the more negative ones, she saw that Adonis was starting to get along better with his teammates and was seemingly more at ease.

In the sixth and penultimate week of the season, Adonis had a breakthrough game in which he scored multiple points and, more importantly, led the team in High Fives and cheering for good plays made by both sides. Kaitlyn was struck by his leadership and decided that she would invite Adonis to join her roster of junior coaches for the last rotation of the school year. However, during the seventh and final week, everything changed and Adonis's behavior tanked. He got in a fight with a teammate and was openly rude to Kaitlyn. After the game when they were presenting participation awards, Adonis got so agitated that he stormed out of the gym.

That evening also happened to be the night before Kaitlyn was scheduled to announce the new junior coach team, and she found herself in a real conundrum. How could she possibly ask Adonis to be a junior coach after the way he'd behaved? But as she thought about it, and tried to imagine what was going on for Adonis, she considered the possibility that he was really just breaking up with volleyball before it broke up with him. She thought about how we were always saying that our job at Playworks is to see the best in every kid so that they can see it for themselves. And so, almost against her better judgment, Kaitlyn decided to add Adonis to her junior coach roster.

The next day when she posted the junior coach list on the school bulletin board, all the kids rushed up to see who had been selected. Everyone, that is, except Adonis. It's easy to imagine that Adonis didn't rush up to the board because in his mind he knew he wasn't on the list—he had controlled that situation, even if that meant getting an outcome he didn't want. It wasn't until all the other kids had filed away that Adonis finally went up to confirm what he knew, and Kaitlyn said you could see him react physically to the shock of seeing his name on the list.

Adonis walked up quickly to Kaitlyn and asked to speak to her outside. She followed him and when she caught up, she could tell that he was having a lot of feelings. "Coach K," he started, shifting from foot to foot. "I just want to thank you for letting me be on your volleyball team." Kaitlyn smiled, and tried to be reassuring, "Of course, Adonis. It was a pleasure to have you on the team!" Adonis looked genuinely surprised. "It was?" he asked.

Kaitlyn said that she knew in that moment that no matter what happened that she had done the right thing making Adonis a junior coach. That no nine-year-old should ever wonder if it was a pleasure for someone to have you on their team.

Power of
Play:

Trust is an essential precondition for building an environment where learning can happen. Playworks has experimented with a number of different ways to contribute to this on the playground. Providing choice and voice—the opportunity to choose the activity that you are going to participate in and to have a say in the activities that are happening and how they feel—stands out. This can be harder to do in the classroom. Letting students decide what they want to study, with whom, where, and when—let alone having a say in the outcomes—is a lot to ask when balanced with all the objectives against which educators are held accountable.

COVID-19 has challenged our understanding of the non-negotiables in education. Play can be instructive in offering ideas for the co-creation of learning opportunities that enable students to lead their own educational experiences. Building trust—between the teacher and student and among the students—is essential for this to be possible.

We build Trust with each other through Play

The Playworks approach to students who are acting out is to give them more attention, with an emphasis on positive attention in the form of additional responsibility. This frequently results in what school leaders experience as a magical transformation of the schoolyard. It is blindingly simple and also incredibly challenging because it requires someone just slightly removed from the school's daily operations who is, nonetheless, present on a daily basis and with the access of someone on the inside. There is a luxury in being the person responsible for recess without any of the other account-ability oversight that comes along with being a teacher—the pressures of meeting academic improvement goals, balancing student needs in the classroom, and covering the prescribed curriculum. The latitude to let a child talk back to you without the danger of it fundamentally undermining your authority creates an opportunity and an opening to respond in a way that does not feel possible for many grown-ups in a school setting.

Having staff members jump into games to model playful participation and offer encouraging words and High Fives to students who are struggling with behavioral expectations can also make a significant difference. By moving from observer or authority on the sidelines to being a player, adults communicate that they believe every student can be a positive contributor to the game. From the student's perspective, experiencing the attention of an involved adult is dramatically different from being monitored.

Another counterintuitive strategy you can try is giving leadership opportunities to kids who are acting out, not necessarily right in the moment when they are disrupting the experience for everyone, but perhaps the next day or later in the week. Responsibilities can include actions such as giving High Fives to every player who gets out or inviting other kids to play who seem tentative about jumping in. Many students will rise to the expectations offered them and are more likely to trust the adults who give them the chance.

Small
Start:

A great activity to start the trust-building process is **Partner Challenge.** Assemble all the participants in a defined space—you can use cones to mark out the space if you're outside in a big area, or the markings on the floor if those are available inside—and introduce the concept of mingling. In Partner Challenge, mingling looks a little bit like a rhumba, with a few steps forward and one back, some fancy arm motions and a sing-song chanting of "Mingle, Mingle, Mingle . . . Mingle, Mingle, Mingle!" Determine a "magic word" for the day (having a different magic word every day has served me well in life) and explain that when you call out that magic word, "Rutabaga!", for example, everyone should freeze, find a partner nearest to them and await further instructions.

Once you have confirmed that everyone has a partner—if there is one extra person, you can either create a group of three or partici-pate yourself—you introduce the opening question/story prompt. These should be adjusted to the age of your group and can get slightly more personal as you progress, but the intention is just to get people sharing, not to prompt huge disclosures of truth. These might include "Take 24 seconds to tell your partner about your favorite game and why," or "Take 19 seconds to tell your partner about your favorite movie, book, or TV show" or "You have one minute to describe the most fun thing that happened to you over the summer."

Generally it works to rotate through three rounds of different part-ners and questions and after each round of questions you create an identity for the partnership—your first partner might be your air High-Five partner, your second partner could be your secret hand-shake partner, and your third partner is your bust-a-dance-move partner—allowing these teams to create their own moves/hand-shakes, and so on, distanced or not as health protocols require. These random partners can also be useful as a tool for quickly creating new groupings as needed throughout the day, as in, "OK, find your air High-Five partner for this next activity."

Fire
in Your Belly

During the 2005–2006 school year Playworks was invited for a visit by the Johns Hopkins Institute for Summer Learning in Baltimore. We made a plan to include some school visits because we were curious to see how recess looked the same and different on the other side of the country.

One of the staff members who joined that trip, a coach named Lamar, accompanied me on a visit to one of the schools. During the meeting with the principal, Mr. Thomasberger, we learned that the school hadn't had recess in almost five years. Lamar had said nothing during the meeting with the principal up until this revelation, but he was suddenly unable to restrain himself. "But what about when the students are done eating lunch?" he asked.
Mr. Thomasberger explained that the students stayed in the lunchroom. "What about the kindergarteners?" Lamar asked, clearly convinced there was something he wasn't getting.
Mr. Thomasberger just shook his head no. Lamar started to ask

another clarifying question, but Mr. Thomasberger cut him off, "We don't have recess. Our students don't know how to play."

And with that comment, everything about Lamar's body language changed. He sat up straighter and declared in a tone that made it clear he wasn't going to take no for an answer, "Let me take your students out for recess today." Mr. Thomasberger made a few half-hearted excuses that Lamar quickly addressed, and a couple of hours later, the principal accompanied us into the cafeteria where about 120 fourth and fifth graders were pretty much bouncing off the walls. There were two lunch ladies stationed at the exits, and they looked alarmed as Lamar strode confidently to the middle of the space and clapped out a rhythm. Mr. Thomasberger nodded to the lunch ladies reassuringly, and although a few students looked over at Lamar, no one really responded. Undaunted, Lamar clapped out another rhythm, and this time a few students tentatively followed suit, while most of the students were now craning their necks to see what was going on. Lamar clapped out a rhythm a third time, and literally all the students repeated the rhythm and the room fell silent.

Using his best playground voice, Lamar introduced himself to the students and explained that he was visiting from California (there was a collective "ohhhh . . ." as if that explained his zany behavior) and that their principal had said it was OK for him to take the students out for recess today. Cheers erupted! "But I'm going to need you to do three things for me—I need you to show your teach-ers and Mr. Thomasberger that you can handle this, so finish up your lunches, clean up, and then line up so that we can all go out to the schoolyard safely."

And just like that, the students did as they were asked and we were headed out to the playground. Once outside, Lamar asked the students to circle up and count off in three groups. We led a couple of different games—Switch and Gaga Ball as I recall—all of which lasted about 10 minutes and then Lamar circled the students back up. After whipping around the circle to share one word each about their experience, Lamar asked the students to show their principal and teachers that they could file back in to class with the same enthusiasm and respectfulness they had summoned on the way out. Lamar looked extraordinarily pleased with himself as the principal shook his hand and thanked him. Unexpectedly and without hesitancy, the two lunch ladies approached Lamar to give him a hug and ask if he would be returning the following day.

Power of
Play:

Although the Lamar story touches on a number of valuable play concepts—the importance of handling transitions, the influence of place—I am most struck by what it says about the power of intrinsic motivation—for Lamar and the students. When I was sitting next to Lamar in that principal's office, I could not help but notice how Lamar was moved by his inner "unreasonable self" in the best possible way. His own love of play, and all of his experiences working with kids and play, made it physically impossible for him to sit by as Mr. Thomasberger explained that their students "didn't know how to play."

And in bringing play to the students that day, Lamar didn't rely exclusively on his own motivation or charisma, he tapped the students' intrinsic motivation as well, asking them to join him as allies, co-conspirators even, in the changemaking work of bringing recess to school that day.

Going back to the work of Stuart Brown, the drive to play is universal among mammals—wolf pups, humans, chimpanzees, you name it. The drive to play is wired into our DNA. We don't have to urge, require or cajole children to engage with each other by playing— they just naturally do it. Taking it one step further, consider that play has survived an epoch's worth of evolutionary pressure. We use play to experiment with behaviors, suffering the natural consequences of poor choices when we're playing, thereby learning which kinds of actions and behaviors work and which don't. Our instinct to play is powerful because the lessons it teaches are so important

I have noted that one of the things that is definitional about play is the presence of volition. You can't really be forced to play. In this regard, play is inherently designed to offer students the opportunity for "choice and voice" in an environment where logistical demands often make that challenging. Still, the presence of choice and voice does not mean that there is no structure and that students can say or do whatever they want. To the contrary, the predictable structure of play—its rules, rituals, and referees—provides valuable opportunities within which students can experiment with their own agency.

Play taps our Intrinsic Motivation

Tapping the intrinsic motivation to keep playing is an effective strategy for changing the dynamic on the playground when it's dysfunctional. More often than not, games on the playground get interrupted by arguments over things like whether the ball was in or out. Kids are eager to get back to playing, and this intrinsic motivation makes them open to the arbitrary nature of Rock-Paper-Scissors (or RoShamBo as described next) to settle those disputes.

To create a norm around using RoShamBo as the all-purpose problem-solver for the inconsequential disagreements that arise, we introduce the tool as a baked-in part of a number of different games, providing a non-didactic way of encouraging that practice. Games such as Switch; RoShamBo Relay; RoShamBo Rockstar; Giants, Wizards, and Elves all make using RoShamBo an automatic response when conflicts arise.

We also see that the experience of tapping intrinsic motivation out on the playground can contribute to its presence in the classroom. A student's willingness to practice a basketball lay-up or dribbling a soccer ball for hours reflects the unarticulated understanding that success is frequently preceded by multiple failed attempts. Translating this understanding into how we do math, how we learn to play the piano, or how we become more comfortable with public speaking is possible when play allows for a shift in identity—"I'm someone who keeps trying" or "I'm someone who's not afraid to make mistakes." This sense of identity can be significantly reinforced by the grown-ups who witness the hours of practice.

Small
Start:

We have found that introducing Rock-Paper-Scissors—or RoShamBo—is a critical first step in getting students to suspend their disbelief that their peers will ever be willing to engage in the basic cooperative activities that make play possible. Admittedly, Playworks has developed an almost religious zeal about this "problem-solving" tool, and that may influence the results, but that's a bit of a chicken-and-egg argument. When Playworks staff members begin programming at a new school, one of the first things they will do is to introduce a handful of games that center around the use of RoShamBo.

Although teaching the rules to Rock-Paper-Scissors may seem reminiscent of explaining how the seatbelt works in an airplane, we think it's equally important. Also, we have some strong feelings about how one does it correctly. Here's how we do it. First, you break into pairs. Then you each put out your non-dominant hand like a table and review the rules—rock, which is a fist, crushes scissors, which is a peace sign on its side; scissors cut paper, which is just your hand out flat; and paper covers rock. You just put your rock, paper, or scissors on your own table—no need to demonstrate crushing someone else's scissors with your rock. Also, we "Show on Bo," so you practice having everyone say "Ro-Sham-Bo" together and you throw out your rock, paper, or scissors as you say "Bo." No "Ro-Sham-Bo-shoot." And finally, and most important, this is not a "best three out of five" situation. You throw again if you throw the same thing (e.g., you both throw rock) but we are firmly of the one-and-done school of RoShamBo, and I think you should be, too.

What
Is Normal?

Nelson Mandela, in the midst of dismantling apartheid in South Africa, observed, "Sport has the power to change the world. It has the power to inspire. It has the power to unite people in a way that little else does. It speaks to youth in a language they understand. Sport can create hope where once there was only despair."[2] Laureus Sport for Good, an international organization inspired by Mandela's work, aims to accelerate this power of sport by highlighting champion athletes—athletes who also demonstrate a commitment to contributing more broadly in society—who serve as Laureus Ambassadors. Over the years Playworks has partnered with Laureus, and in spring 2015 the Paralympic athlete Bob Lujano visited Sheridan Elementary in Minneapolis, a Playworks school, to celebrate his Laureus induction. Bob, who had both of his arms and legs amputated as a result of a rare blood disease, is a Paralympic bronze medalist, was the president of US Quad Rugby, and was featured in the documentary movie *Murderball*.

When Bob showed up at Sheridan and rolled through the halls in his wheelchair, the children noticed. And, as children will do, they commented audibly about his absence of arms and legs. Once circled up in the auditorium, Bob and I began throwing the rugby ball back and forth, and the kids' comments turned quickly into questions. "How can you throw and catch without hands?" Bob explained that his arms had been amputated right at the elbow and that his father had helped to design special rubber sleeves that enabled him to grip things. "You're an athlete?" Bob explained that he had won a bronze medal in the Paralympic Games, and then he went on to talk more about the games and Quad Rugby in response to other questions. Although the grown-ups in the room remained visibly uneasy—presumably anxious that the students were going to say something "wrong"—the students quickly shifted to a state of acceptance. After 10 minutes of questions and 20 minutes of rugby drills, Bob circled the kids back up and asked if any of the students had friends or family members that had a disability. All sorts of hands shot up and one little girl, unable to control her excitement, shouted out with tremendous pride, "My mom is deaf!"

Power of
Play:

The way values show up in any environment is often reflected in—and reinforced by—that community's social norms. Social norms are the unwritten rules of beliefs, attitudes, and behaviors that are considered acceptable in a particular social group or culture. Social norms are often quite small things—shaking hands when you meet someone or giving out High Fives when someone gets out in Four Square. They vary with different cultures, for example, making eye contact is a sign of respect in some cultures and shows impudence in others. And they are often unspoken. How did we learn that you face forward in an elevator? Consider for a moment just how profoundly unsettling it is—or might be if you've never had the experience—to ride in an elevator when someone you didn't know was facing the wrong way. Play is a critical developmental tool for learning social norms, and it is affected by, and a determinant of, these accepted practices.

As children, we get many of our cues about what is expected of us from play, and this directly affects our sense of identity. When are we supposed to be quiet and when are we allowed to be loud and boisterous? Who plays which games? Who is good at what? Do the rules apply equally to everyone? What are the rules for kids who look like me? For my grade level? My gender? My race? We have an opportunity to practice with a variety of different roles through play, and social norming can either reinforce an openness to this experimentation or suggest its limits. Social norming is inextricably tied to how we respond to the expectations of others, which in turn directly effects how social roles are chosen and assigned. Along these lines, play can change how we view and interact with others—for better and worse—and this has huge implications for schools. When social norming encourages trust and vulnerability, deep learning is more likely to happen.

Karl Groos, the German philosopher and naturalist, applied evolutionary theory to the study of play very early on. He identified play activity as practice for developing the skills and competencies that would enable "higher animals" to master the tasks of life.[3] He also wrote at length about "imitative play" in humans, whereby children expanded on the behaviors of adults. Interestingly, Groos suggested that you could determine how different animals—humans included—might play by understanding the behaviors that would best help a species survive and reproduce. Groos was one of the earliest theorists to make the connection that play had survived evolution, despite being a risky behavior, because it set young animals up to succeed.

This concept of imitative play is perhaps the clearest example of how play relates to the establishment of social norms in good and bad ways. Over the years Playworks staff members have recounted stories of young children starting up games that involved saving peers from catastrophes, as well as constructing less generous, yet equally elaborate, storylines that focused on excluding others. Our children are watching us, hungry for cues about how to respond to different situations, how to treat one another, and how to make meaning of the world around us. No parents who have ever watched their young daughter or son playing an imaginative game of house or work or school, has failed to notice the bits of language and actions borrowed from older siblings or other family members that are peppered throughout their child's running monologue.

Healthy communities use Play to instill Positive Social Norms

Beyond imitation, children's play reflects adult encouragement—even if that encouragement is provided unwittingly. If students are consistently behaving in a certain way, there is a tremendous likelihood that grown-ups have created some sort of structural incentive that motivates this behavior. A frequent example of this can be found in "attention-getting" behavior, which is perhaps best served by being reinterpreted as connection-seeking behavior. Just like in the story with Mrs. Peyton at Santa Fe Elementary I shared in the Introduction, one of the most common scenarios that Playworks has encountered over the years when arriving at a new school is a recess culture in which two or three students are stirring up trouble on a daily basis. We consistently find that this behavior is pretty easily redirected by preemptively offering positive attention, suggesting that the behaviors that at first blush might seem "bad" are really just an unfortunate expression of a desire for connection.

Once the students who are spearheading the negative behaviors have been co-opted, building trust among students requires giving them the tools they need to solve their own conflicts. We've talked about RoShamBo in the previous Big Change. Another strategy we have used to great effect (and are now adapting because of social distancing requirements) are High Fives and encouraging the reckless use of "Good Job! Nice Try!"

Small
Start:

It's easy to be a bit skeptical about the effectiveness of **High Fives** and actively encouraging kids to say **"Good Job, Nice Try!"** whenever someone gets out. And lest you worry that everyone who works at Playworks is cynicism-proof, you should know that we do make fun of ourselves in doing it. But all that aside, actively working to shift what kids say and do when someone makes a mistake while playing makes a huge difference in the experience. Here's where the Buddhist concept of intention intersects with recess: just having kids go through the motions of saying "Good job! Nice try!" eventually makes it become sincere. Four Square is a great example because every round involves someone "getting out," so in lieu of everyone shouting "you're out," everyone says "Good job! Nice try!" The person gets High Fives from their fellow players and heads to the back of the Recycle Line and the game keeps going. Although there may be some snark in the tone of some people when the practice is first put in place, it turns out that snark is pretty hard to hold on to and it dissipates.

A quick note about High Fives in this COVID moment: although we are hopeful that human contact will once again be a normal and non-worrisome thing, for the time being we are creatively exploring air High Fives and invite you to join us in adding celebratory spins to the gesture.

Time-Out:
Keystone Activity

A few years ago my friend David Bornstein introduced me to a concept in biology called a keystone species—an organism that helps define an entire ecosystem, without which an ecosystem would be dramatically different or cease to exist altogether. The story of the gray wolf in Yellowstone is sometimes held up as a great example of how a keystone species affects an ecosystem. When the park was first opened, the federal government launched a devastatingly successful extermination campaign against the wolf to protect neighboring livestock that set off a chain of reactions dramatically changing the environment. Lacking an apex predator, the elk population exploded, leading to overgrazing which in turn dramatically affected the region's plant and animal species. In the 1990s the federal government reintroduced the gray wolf to Yellowstone to astounding effect: the elk population has diminished and populations of the other animals, along with the plants and birds, have almost fully recovered.

When David told me about the keystone species, he shared that he'd been thinking about play as a keystone activity, and ever since then I've thought that it provides one of the best frameworks I've encountered for explaining the many ways play is linked to a wide range of outcomes and developmental changes for kids. When healthy play is present in a school it fundamentally shifts the school culture and climate in ways that profoundly influence the larger ecosystem—from school attendance to behavior in the classroom, from how students and staff members interact to how students treat their classmates and students in other grades. When play is withheld, not only do individual students lose the opportunity to build the multiple skills that they need as individuals navigating the world but also the larger community loses the much-needed experiential opportunities to practice the skills of collaboration, cooperation, and conflict resolution that effective teaching and learning require.

Anyone
Can Play

When Tara Doherty first started out as a coach at Fairmont Elementary School in El Cerrito, California, the special education classes were kept separate from the mainstream classes during recess. Working with the school principal and the special education instructor, Tara was able to incorporate some of the students with developmental disabilities into her Junior Coach program. This new approach dramatically shifted the entire recess experience, blending the classes and the patterns of play that followed. Although the staff members supported Tara in this work, she did have to overcome some skepticism initially. Adults at the school wondered if the mainstreamed students would take instruction from the students in special education. In the end, not only did the mainstream students follow their lead on the playground, the shift served both groups of students by undoing some of the messages inherent in the previous segregation.

Power of
Play:

A useful way to think about inclusion—as opposed to equity or diversity or belonging—is as an active invitation to participate. Grown-ups frequently marvel at how "easily" young children will make new friends and start playing with complete strangers. In mere moments, deeply involved fantasy games can spontaneously emerge among kids who hardly know one another, with elaborate storylines and complicated narratives that the children co-create while running up the slide or hiding behind a tree.

Play is often way more fun with other players, and so it is natural for students to encourage their peers to join in. When this invitation is delivered consistently and repeatedly to each person individually, then members of the community come to believe that they are always welcome and thus are more likely to fully enjoy the experience of school in a whole new way. Not incidentally, our approach to addressing bullying behaviors works very much along these same lines: incentivizing actions that promote kindness and inclusion is more effective as a preventative measure to crowd out bullying behaviors than having to build reactive practices for environments where these bullying behaviors are unwittingly encouraged.

This standing invitation to be a part of whatever happens is a critical foundation to creating an environment where people experience a sense of belonging—where they are not just invited but granted the full rights of engagement, including, most notably, the right to suggest how the experience might be improved. Because of play's inherently adaptive nature—by virtue of the fact that it is an activity undertaken for no apparent purpose—it is uniquely well designed to afford the adjustments required to make it possible for literally anyone to be a part. Someone's in a wheelchair? No problem, the space is expanded to make room for a wheelchair to maneuver. Someone's slower than someone else? They start closer to the end line. In play, you can always create different roles in the game that allow for different abilities to shine through.

Translating this commitment to adaptation in the classroom and elsewhere in life may seem like an artificial approach to the "real world," but in truth the real world is actually much more of a hybrid of competition and cooperation than we usually acknowledge. Our collective response to the COVID-19 pandemic has been a perfect example of this, with the recognition that "we keep each other safe" being demonstrated time and time again. One of the most powerful lessons of play is that we are reliant on one another—our teammates, our coaches, our opponents—for a great game. This is the truth of our messy interdependence.

We feel Included through Play

Playworks defines *inclusion* as "actively encouraging and ensuring dynamic participation for all children, staff, and involved community regardless of abilities and/or past experiences." We pay attention to patterns of play on the schoolyard—are groups mixed by age, ethnicity, ability, and gender? It can be a challenge balancing student choice and control over what, and with whom, they play with the desire to create an inclusive playground. We have found that when our staff members norm inviting others to play and participate in games that model inclusivity, we are able to create environments where inclusion is a shared value.

This is another place where the power of showing as opposed to telling is really evident. Because Playworks coaches get in the game and model inclusion, rather than only instructing kids to include others from the sidelines, the practice is more easily translated into a social norm, reinforced by the more joyful experience of having more people with whom to play.

Small
Start:

Celebrating accomplishments and expressing gratitude for people's efforts is a great way to include everyone. At Playworks we have tried to creatively encourage this practice through the ritual of **Claps**. The **Whoosh Clap** is the granddaddy of claps. The person who is being appreciated—the Whoosh Clap beneficiary—is asked to stand up in front of the group. The leader—this can be a grown-up or a student—counts to three and on three everyone claps and then gathers a big ball of invisible energy that they "throw" at the beneficiary while making a "whooshing" noise. It's very *Matrix* and the beneficiary is encouraged to visibly and playfully respond to the experience of all that energy being thrown in her direction.

Over the years the Playworks staff have created an immense cata-logue of claps and people invent new claps all the time. As the practice gets more established, you can ask whoever is being appreciated to choose their favorite clap. Other claps include the Looking Good! Clap, the Beautiful Clap, the New York Taxi Driver Clap, and the Make It Rain Clap.[4]

If at First
You Don't
Succeed . . .

6

When Playworks was still Sports4Kids, we experimented with starting a girls' basketball league. This was over 20 years ago, long before you might see college women's basketball on television and way before the idea for the WNBA had any traction.

I have a vivid memory from one Thursday night toward the end of that first season when one of the smaller girls found herself in possession of the ball right as the clock was counting down. She hadn't scored—or even taken a shot—previously during the season, and she was clearly not thinking that this was the moment to start. She was looking around desperately for someone to pass the ball to, but everyone else was being tightly guarded and her teammates were all shouting, "Shoot! Shoot!" Watching her as she squared up and launched the ball with all her might toward the basket, I could imagine what she was feeling in that moment. It seemed as though the whole gym fell silent as the ball soared through the air in an improbable arc that swished through the hoop, nothing but net! There was a beat longer of silence and then the entire gym erupted in cheers from both sides. I have no doubt that that moment is indelibly imprinted in her memory.

Power of
Play:

Play is the original amateur activity, and I use that word with the utmost respect. It is funny how the word has almost come to be a slur, as in "You amateur . . ." but the root of the word is from the Latin *amare,* "to love." Being a beginner at something can be either an extraordinarily wonderful thing—the excitement of a whole new world opening up—or an overwhelming and daunting experience. Healthy play has the power to help shift things toward the positive. But it matters how it feels.

This is a critical understanding that we will come back to time and again in this book: *it matters how it feels.* To get and keep a really great game going, you need the least-skilled player on the field as much as you need the best one. Given their relative experiences of the game—it can be hard to enjoy things that we are not good at—it makes a lot of sense to design the game to maximize the joy of the less-skilled so that, lacking the glory, they are incentivized to keep playing. The existence of a strong community makes a huge difference in the experience of "enjoying something that we are not good at," which is basically another way of describing learning.

We find joy in being a Beginner

Learning is inherently inefficient, and play motivates us to stick with it long after common sense might suggest we quit. Learning is also inherently vulnerable. Education is not possible without a willingness to experience repeated failure, and play represents an extraordinary opportunity to center the love that motivates the amateur.

One of the core tools Playworks staff members employ in creating a comfort with being a beginner is scaffolding. Scaffolding involves breaking down a game or challenge into a series of activities that enable students to develop a level of comfort with the component parts. Although this might be initially met with some resistance by students who claim to already have significant expertise, our experience is that not infrequently the students who protest the loudest are mostly posturing, and ultimately they appreciate the opportunity to learn more about a game they love. If you take basketball as an example, scaffolding might look like a dribbling relay race, a game of Triangle Tag to practice boxing out, and Three Lines Basketball to focus on passing followed by Knockout.

Small
Start:

For the youngest players—and for teachers who are new to incorporating play—**Sequence Touch** is a great game for making it fun to be a beginner while inviting participants to be fully present. While standing in a circle, the leader explains that the object of the game is to do three things while the leader counts down from 10 and to then return to their original spot without bumping into anyone. For example, the leader might ask that everyone touch something red with their elbow, something black with their foot, and something green with their knee. The leader checks to confirm that everyone understands the instructions and reminds them again of the three objectives—red with your elbow, black with your foot, and green with your knee. They then say the magic word and count down as the participants set about achieving their three goals.

Sequence Touch allows for the leader and the players to practice with giving and following instructions, encourages students to practice moving their bodies through space while being aware of others, and helps teach body parts and colors—all in a way that is intuitive and taps the students' intrinsic motivation to play.

Follow
the Leader

Erin Lewellen, currently COO of Global Citizen Year, started her career with Playworks as a coach. She is fond of telling a story about being out on the playground at Hawthorne Elementary—one of Oakland's biggest elementary schools at the time with 1,200 K–5 students—when she noticed an administrator from the district looking a bit lost. She approached to see if she could help. "Is there a fair happening here today?" he asked. Erin shook her head, "No, this is just recess." He still seemed confused. "But there are so many different activities and all the kids are participating. *Who's in charge*?" Erin scanned the yard to see what he was seeing and indeed her junior coaches did have a dozen different games set up across the massive blacktop, essential to keeping the more than 300 students present engaged. Erin had to laugh as she responded, "I'd have to say the students are in charge."

Retelling this story almost 20 years later, Erin is still struck by the common adult misconception that kids are incapable of self-organizing. Yes, they need some skills and experience to do so well—like anyone—but mostly they need the latitude to learn. Play creates that opportunity.

Power of
Play:

Play is essential to leadership development—for young people and adults—in its ability to provide an experiential proving ground for resilience, trust, listening, and empathy. It creates a place for us to build our own skills leading and being led and to understand the interplay of these two activities. It enables us to experiment with—and learn about—our own leadership style while not taking our-selves so ridiculously seriously as to completely discourage anyone who might be willing to follow. It also creates an opportunity to explore and come to understand the many facets of leadership—from the demands of servant leadership to the expressions of unreasonableness that lead to changemaking and the responsibili-ties and expectations that accompany the power and influence that we more traditionally associate with the idea of leadership. Ultimately, play stands out as a powerful tool for leadership develop-ment because it is grounded in the importance of belonging and derives its power and influence from a coalition of the willing with an aim of benefitting the common good.

Play is where we Practice Leadership (the new kind)

Historically, our societal attitudes toward leadership and change-making haven't been particularly democratic. Past attitudes extoll leadership as being exemplified by hierarchy and control. Daniel Goleman's 1995 book, *Emotional Intelligence,* was groundbreaking in its framing of the importance of an individual's capacity to tune in to their emotions as a strong determinant of success, calling out five key elements: self-awareness, self-regulation, motivation, empathy, and social skills.[5] His later book, *Primal Leadership,* built on this early exploration of emotional intelligence by connecting inspiring and effective leadership with the presence of these attributes.[6]

Also tied up in vestigial attitudes about power and hierarchy is the often unspoken assumption that leadership is a rare and inherent skill. In the book *Everyone Leads: Building Leadership from the Community Up*, former Playworks board member Paul Schmitz demonstrates through a variety of historic and contemporary examples that "everyone can step up and take responsibility for influencing and working with others for common goals."[7]

Goleman's and Schmitz's perspectives on leadership emphasize and celebrate the qualities that can be developed through play. Self-awareness, self-regulation, motivation, empathy, and social skills are the natural by-products of healthy play environments. These are skills that support the development of communities in which all participants see themselves as having a role and responsibility in achieving what is best for the larger group. Another way of framing this ideal is through the concept of belonging. john a. powell explains: "Belonging means more than just being seen. Belonging entails having a meaningful voice and the opportunity to participate in the design of social and cultural structures. Belonging means having the right to contribute to, and make demands on, society and political institutions."[8]

One of the biggest "a-ha's" to emerge from identifying student playground leaders is that leadership can take a variety of different forms. There are lots of leadership programs out there, and far too many of them cater to the kids that you would expect—the "good students" and the "well-behaved" kids, with all that is fraught and problematic about those labels. I experienced this firsthand in elementary school when I was a crossing guard—resplendent with the neon orange Sam Browne belt. One of the things that distinguishes the leadership opportunities offered through play is that it's not just available to the usual suspects.

At Playworks, we have often joked that sometimes "kids use their superpowers for good, and sometimes not so much." It could be argued that using one's superpowers to lead others to break the rules inherently requires more creativity, charisma, and initiative. Playworks staff members have repeatedly discovered that identifying the students who were leading others to be disruptive and engaging them as leaders in making recess fun, inclusive, and safe not only dramatically shifts the experience of recess and the overall school culture but also directly affects the participating students' sense of self.

Over the years, Playworks coaches have gone to great lengths to outdo one another in terms of selecting students who were the least likely candidates. Although this has sometimes been motivated by the hubris of youth, the results have been overwhelmingly positive—a good reminder that the leadership of young adults can be important in reimagining our existing systems and that inexperience is as often a strength as it is a liability.

Although our staff's willingness to make the initial leap in recognizing the inherent leadership ability of all students is a critical piece of this shift, play itself is an essential ingredient. So much of how schools are structured reflects an understandable, but problematic, instinct to exert control over students. Precisely because play affords children the opportunity to experience a sense of agency in the midst of this, it creates a theater for practicing the same skills that enable them to become strong self-advocates and changemakers. The most effective leaders combine this sense of agency with an equal presence of empathy.

Erin's experience of supporting her Hawthorne students to self-organize games out at recess feels like a giant example of how distributed leadership can work. By providing people with the training and support they need and believing in their inherent ability to do so, it is possible to create an extended network of support designed for maximum engagement. It doesn't mean that there is no organizational structure, no hierarchy, or that everything is decided by consensus. Play values rules, rituals, and referees in a way that supports leadership development because it compels us to consider the elements of the experience that need to be consistent, investigate where adaptation can happen, and discover the optimal structure to ensure a balance between the two.

A tradition at Playworks is a variation on the theme of TED-like talks that we call Playing with Words. Joy Weiss, former Playworks board chair and the president and CEO of Tempo Automation, whose smart manufacturing platform revolutionizes the way companies bring electronic products to market, gave one such talk at a Playworks national board gathering. In her talk, she compared the skills that our Junior Coaches learn with the skills needed to be a successful executive in the business world. She called out the ways that play helped to impart the 4 Cs of 21st-century skills: critical thinking, communication, collaboration, and creativity. She described visiting a school and being introduced to a Junior Coach who welcomed her, introduced himself, and asked probing questions about Joy's relationship to Playworks and the role of a board member. This Junior Coach described how he and the other students shared responsibility for overseeing playground activities and the challenges and frustrations that having the other kids not listen could cause. He talked about various problem-solving tools they employed to resolve the inevitable conflicts that arose. He conveyed a genuine pride in his role, a sense of responsibility to his school and his classmates, and, most strikingly to Joy, a profound sense of confidence in not only his own abilities but also in the collective capacity of his fellow students to make things work. He was, in Joy's words, exactly whom she would want to hire as an executive at her company. And he was nine.

If there is one element of the Playworks program that I would call out as our "special sauce," it would be the Junior Coach program, which gives kids the opportunity to self-organize and learn leadership skills. It is also, I believe, an extraordinary example of how play creates essential experiential learning opportunities that help kids become drivers of their own educations and the changemakers of the future.

Our Junior Coach program emerged in our second year of existence, conceived of by former staffer Kate Hobbs as a response to work she had been doing with youth through a program she had cofounded called Destiny Arts. At Destiny, martial arts and dance are used to promote leadership and build community across difference, but in her conversations with students, Sifu Kate (as they called her at Destiny) was constantly hearing that although the things they were learning were true at Destiny, they didn't apply at school.

Working with a group of 12 students, Kate built the foundation of the Junior Coach program that would be enhanced by other Playworks staff members over the years. Since then the Junior Coach curriculum has expanded to include explorations of the characteristics of leadership that students see and value in their community, exploration of their own aspirations as leaders, and concrete leadership skill-building activities that are reinforced through their application out at recess. Although the Playworks leadership training is done largely through games and play, it is nonetheless rigorous and respectful of students' inherent capacity to lead. Observing a Junior Coach training, I was blown away by the students' ability to explain and demonstrate the difference between "aggressive" and "assertive" communication, and their own insights about the role of a leader as someone who supports others in developing the skills of being a self-advocate.

Small
Start:

A great game that helps students develop the leadership skills of empathy, problem-solving, teamwork, and social awareness is **Toxic Waste Dump.** One of the most striking things about the Junior Coach experience is how it teaches students that leadership isn't a solitary experience—that they need not only the cooperation of the students whom they are hoping to lead, but also the collaboration of their fellow Junior Coaches. Toxic Waste Dump requires a marked start and finish line along with some cardboard, carpet squares, or another somewhat indestructible object that the players can easily stand on and carry. The leader explains that the area between the start and finish lines is a vast pool of toxic sludge, with the object of the game being to get all the players from the starting line to the finish line without touching the ground. Players can only be in the toxic sludge if they are standing on an item provided. If a player steps off and into the sludge, they must all return to the starting line. If an item is placed into the toxic sludge without being constantly touched by a player, the whole team must return back to the starting line and that object is no longer available to help them get across.

Toxic Waste Dump is best understood as an exercise in collaboration and problem-solving, so the leader wants to be sure to encourage the team to start the activity by coming up with a strategy to try that will get all of their teammates across the playing area safely without stepping in the toxic sludge. You'll also want to interject with brainstorming strategies during the activity if the team gets stuck, giving examples if needed to help the students build these skills. The goal is to model the kind of respectful support that you hope young leaders will offer their fellow students, allowing them to wrestle with the challenge while also setting them up to succeed.

Emotional
Rescue

8

When Playworks participated in a randomized control evaluation of our impact, one of the most notable findings was that teachers rated bullying in Playworks schools significantly lower than in schools where we were not present. In media interviews about the study, I was asked repeatedly about what we did to "stop the bullies." I would attempt to explain that we focused on building an environment that crowded out the bullying behaviors by creating other opportunities for students to get attention, reinforced by expectations around how games would operate and how people would treat one another. My answers were apparently unsatisfying to the interviewers, who seemed to all want a juicier story about bullies being vanquished. They didn't want to hear about bullying behaviors, they wanted to talk about individual bullies. My insistence that the humans they were talking about were actually eight-, nine-, and 10-year-old children and that kids behaving in socially unacceptable ways was often the result of adult influence made me a disappointing interview.

Power of
Play:

Bullying behaviors absolutely deserve and demand attention, however the adult desire to address these behaviors in a reactionary way, as opposed to understanding and addressing the underlying conditions that prompt these behaviors, is an extension of how we tend to deal with safety issues. Although not how we usually think of it, one of the most important goals of school safety should be in figuring out how to create an environment that supports and allows for vulnerability.

Dr. Will Massey has thought a lot about the impact of play on kids and its importance. He's an assistant professor and researcher based at Oregon State University (OSU) whose research focuses on the intersection of play, physical health, and child development. In conjunction with studying Playworks, he tested the Great Recess Framework, a validated observational tool that enables schools and researchers to better understand, evaluate, and plan school recess.[9] When I interviewed Will during the COVID-19 lockdown, his thinking on the subject was less academic and most definitely influenced by the challenges of working from home with three kids ages five, six, and 11.

The thing that struck me most in talking with Will was the way the experience of COVID-19 had influenced his thinking on the issue of safety and how kid and adult attitudes on the subject diverged. "If you ask kids directly," he explained, "there's a real gap between what adults and kids think about the adult role. Adults focus on safety. Kids find this incredibly annoying. They want to take risks. They just wish there were more rules about how kids treat each other. They want the adults to intervene there."

It Matters How it Feels

It isn't uncommon that an initial site visit to a school includes overhearing a student making a comment that is unkind or that involves name-calling, or observing exclusionary or bullying behaviors that the adults present seem to conveniently miss. It is an understandable, and quintessentially human, impulse to avoid dealing with these complex issues. Many educators feel unprepared and ill-equipped to address head-on racism, homophobia, religious intolerance, sexism—or any of the other –"isms." They may also not even hear something said as being offensive because so much of our culture is set up to excuse bad behavior by the dominant groups. Responses like "boys will be boys" or "she didn't mean it. . . ." become hardwired in our brains.

We ask that our staff members be the ones who turn toward these complex dynamics, asking for help from the other adults in their schools, being willing to be vulnerable themselves in acknowledging that these are difficult issues that trigger lots of feelings. Our staff members understand their responsibility to model for students a caring, respectful commitment to creating an emotionally healthy learning environment.

There are some simple ways to set a positive emotional tone that if repeated daily are easy to maintain. For example, giving a High Five as a daily greeting to students communicates "Welcome! I'm glad you are here," and knowing each child's name and using their name to share positive feedback when they are participating and following the social norms are strategies for establishing trust. That trust makes a big difference in the moments when things aren't going well. Sharing critical feedback with a child who is out of alignment with expectations is much more productive when the relationship and trust are already there. These small playful gestures consistently confirm that you care.

Small
Start:

Although we talk a lot about rules at school, we don't always make a point of establishing the rules for how we are going to treat one another. Sometimes this is handled as a Classroom Charter, or

Group Agreements. At Playworks, we endeavor to make these commitments somewhat playful. Here are some examples:

- Try It On—Be willing to do something—at least once—even if you think you're not going to enjoy it, and be open to the possibility that you might be wrong!
- Step Up/Step Back—If you are someone who doesn't usually speak up, try and push yourself to actively participate a bit more, and if you are someone who feels very comfortable talking, make sure to check that you're not crowding out others.
- Don't Yuck My Yum—Be respectful of other people's feelings by not criticizing games or thoughts or ideas that differ from your own.
- Take Care of Yourself—Notice what you need and make sure you have it.
- One Mic—During a discussion only one person should be talking at a time so that everyone can hear what the person has to say.
- Have Fun—Boom!

I Disagree!

When Playworks first launched in New Orleans a few years after Hurricane Katrina, a number of the temporary schools that had been built were essentially portable classrooms connected by raised outdoor walkways. For Coach Sean, one of our first-year coaches in Louisiana, this meant that getting from one side of his schoolyard to the other involved a very indirect crossing of the elevated walkways that added considerable difficulty points to overseeing recess. Sean's strategy for dealing with the bifurcated yard involved a well-trained and well-organized crew of Junior Coaches, including a young man named Muhammed. Although Muhammed had a history of getting into scuffles prior to Coach Sean's arrival, he had been on his best behavior since the opportunity to be a Junior Coach had presented itself. Sean was feeling very pleased with his development as a leader.

One day, however, Sean heard ominous noises coming from the other side of the playground and so he started to make the long trek over. As he was winding his way he could see Muhammed running over to address the melee that had formed and after

Why Play Works: Big Changes Start Small

initially being pleased that he was going to help break things up, Sean became worried as Muhammed disappeared into the middle of the crowd of students. Sean picked up his pace as he approached, and he got increasingly worried as he heard the students crying out, "Oooh!" "No way!" and "Again! Again! Again!"

It wasn't until Sean was almost right on top of the students that he realized that Muhammed was in the middle of the scrum presiding over a heated match of RoShamBo between the two disputants—both of whom were repeatedly throwing Rock!

Power of Play:

We are living in an extraordinarily polarized age. At the root of the dysfunction this creates is our inability to be respectful and tolerant in our disagreements and conflict. Our relationship to professional sports is an interesting extension of this dynamic, reflecting how sports can bring us together as Nelson Mandela noted, but also how it can pit us against one another. Nevertheless, on balance, healthy play provides an exceptional opportunity to help children develop a relationship with conflict that contributes to a sense of optimism about the existence of solutions and the power of mutualism—the understanding that mutual well-being is necessary to social well-being.

Having established practices—rituals like RoShamBo that everyone has agreed to use when conflicts arise—tends to ease anticipatory anxiety, reinforcing the message that the existence of conflict is not necessarily a problem. Normalizing conflict and giving students the tools and resilience to address it are among play's most important contributions.

As children are learning to resolve disagreements while playing, they are building a sense of themselves as capable of handling conflict that will serve them, and everyone with whom they disagree. This is the foundation for addressing our fears and worries about conflict, and it is ultimately critical to building the necessary muscles to respond when the stakes get more serious.

BIG CHANGE #9

We can get better at Conflict through Play

There is a moment out on the playground when a Junior Coach understands for the first time that he or she has the power to help other students resolve their conflicts. You can almost watch the process unfold in the young person's head as he or she briefly considers asking a nearby grown-up for help, but instead turns to the students involved and announces "RoShamBo!" It's not offered as a question, or even a suggestion, but rather as a solution—an acknowledgment that "daylight is burning" and time wasted arguing is time not spent playing. It's also a profound collective leadership moment endorsed by all the other kids whose play is otherwise hijacked by the students with the unresolved issue.

For the students who have a disagreement, the face-saving nature of the game—the very arbitrariness of it—is a much-needed distraction that helps them break free of all the baggage that conflict brings with it. Being right or wrong, strong or weak, popular or not—all of it becomes immediately irrelevant. And although to adult eyes it may seem like a fleeting and insignificant moment, our experience is that resolving minor conflicts this way is habit forming and instructive for students who are learning to discern between major and minor conflicts and building the skills to navigate both.

Small
Start:

There are lots and lots of games that center RoShamBo, and one of my favorite games is **Switch.** Switch requires at least five students ideally, four standing on the marked corners of a square and one at the center, with whoever else is waiting to play standing in the Recycle Line. To start a round, the student at the center calls out "Switch," signaling that the four corner-standers need to abandon their respective spots for one of the other corners. The center person is also seeking a spot on a corner, leading to an almost inevitable tie in arriving at one of the spots. This is then decided by a round of RoShamBo. Being compelled to use of the tool as an automatic part of the game creates an entirely different energy in it, and in a non-didactic way sets up the expectation that in play there will be inconsequential conflicts that need to be resolved as quickly as possible so that *we can keep playing*. As soon as the four corner-standers are determined, the person who didn't get a spot gets a High Five and joins the Recycle Line as the first person in line comes in to be the middle Switch-caller.

There are also some really fun variations on Switch, including blowing up the court so that it's really big (like doing it using the four corners of a basketball court), using more than four corners for bigger games that include more people, or calling out different means of transportation (hop, skip, or walk like a penguin).

Time-Out:
Joy + Fear

Barry Svigals is an architect who has been, as he puts it, "designing simultaneously for fear and joy" for the past decade. Hired as the architect for the new school in Newtown, Connecticut, built in the wake of the Sandy Hook shooting, Barry has been at the forefront of the movement to look more critically at how we make schools safe. Televised coverage of gun violence—from Columbine to Sandy Hook—has created the "Columbine generation"—a cohort of young people who have only known a world in which gun violence was an ever-present threat and a defining concern for school administrators that was essentially unknown only 30 years ago.

Barry is quick to point out that although "mass shootings" are understandably terrifying for families everywhere, it is still a relatively unlikely occurrence relative to other threats, such as bullying behaviors and self-harm. In 2019, it was over 200 times more likely that a student would take his or her own life than have it lost in an incident of school violence.[10]

In his work with the Stanford d.school K12 Lab, Barry has had the chance to expand on his thinking on reimagining school safety, incorporating the implications of COVID-19, with Lab co-director sam seidel. They write:

> The notion of school safety is often only concerned with physical harm, but true safety is much more complex. Measures we take to "harden" our schools' perimeters to protect from external attackers, can scare and isolate students and families while failing to address

the more serious issues of wellbeing. The steps we take to protect against the threat of infection may traumatize students and teachers missing the affect it has on how they feel. It doesn't have to be this way.[11]

Thinking about the process of designing simultaneously for fear and joy through the lens of play basically comes down to translating what is required in the moment into rules that promote engagement. Ideally this is achieved through co-creation by the participants to ensure buy-in and accountability, as opposed to simply compliance. Compliance is rarely joyful. When framed in this way—bringing a playful mindset to encouraging safety—it is possible to imagine a more cooperative set of measures built on the understanding that we keep each other safe.

Who Says "Winner Takes All"? 10

In contrast to basketball or soccer or football, most students at Playworks schools have never played volleyball before, and only a few have ever even seen it. As a result, volleyball essentially has no baggage—no gender or racial identity to volleyball (i.e., jump rope = girls; football = boys; soccer = Latinx; basketball = Black). So, when Playworks launched our volleyball league, we started with Newcomb, the modified version of volleyball that allows for catching the ball. We ran it as a co-ed activity. The students were pretty evenly bad at it to start so they visibly improved—across all abilities—as the season progressed. With volleyball, the propensity to get caught up in self-consciousness about not being particularly skilled never took hold, probably because there were so many distractions—learning to rotate, figuring out how to serve, the ritual of giving Low Fives between every point regardless of the outcome, all while counting the number of hits on each side, not to exceed three but ideally more than one.

The family members in attendance at our volleyball games were similarly unfamiliar and that contributed to the overall ease as well. There was no narrative about anyone's child growing up to be a volleyball superstar. The adults in attendance weren't clear enough on the rules to debate a call, and the learning curve was so steep that any time either team had a series of successful hits that resulted in the ball actually going back over the net, the fans were genuinely thrilled and cheered indiscriminately. With everyone getting caught up in the experience, it was the perfect example of how much we need one another for a good game.

Power of
Play:

I once had a conversation with my friend Dave Wish, the founder and CEO of the nonprofit music organization Little Kids Rock, in which he raised the question, "Do we have school orchestras to produce great music, or to encourage student participation?" I was struck by the implications of this question—not only for school music programs, or even for school sports programs, but more broadly in terms of how we design education. When we are making competition a part of the student experience, it's important to ask the question *to what end?* It's not that it's never appropriate, but ultimately competition should be included as a part of our educational system as a means of enhancing the experience, not hindering it.

Play holds an important role in introducing healthy competition to children and for creating experiences that enable people to learn to deal gracefully with winning and losing. Although introducing competitive play at Playworks has sometimes felt a bit fraught, it has also been a source of tremendous excitement and joy. We have intentionally incorporated competition in our choices of activities because it is a real thing that we all need to learn to deal with, and play provides opportunities to experience it in a more gradual manner and in lower stakes environments.

Ultimately, we've also included it because we believe—and have experienced—competition as fun. Winning is extra fun, but playing and losing can also be fun. And, when not fun, at least valuable as an opportunity to learn and grow. Figuring out how to share this awareness with children feels like an important grown-up responsibility that we haven't always honored.

Play is the foundation of Healthy Competition

In the first section of this book, I talked a bit about the difference between play and sport, with the biggest difference ultimately coming down to the goal of winning and the role of competition. Juxtaposing play and sport in this way raises an interesting question: is it possible to have competition when the goal isn't exclusively about winning? Running our leagues has provided a tremendous opportunity to explore this question because we introduce competition in a controlled environment. This enables us to intentionally design the experience to focus on skills-building and teamwork and to bake in rituals to remind everyone involved of the importance of being kind, treating each other with respect, and not losing one's sense of humor. Nonetheless, it hasn't always been easy. One of the recurring themes from interviews with former staff members was how frustrating it was to watch students spin out over their perceptions of winning and losing, negatively shaping their attitudes about different activities, their peers, and themselves.

To address this, Playworks has developed lots of different games where the experience of getting "out" doesn't mean you have to stop playing. Instead of being out, students can do five jumping jacks or five "I'm awesome" moves before jumping back into the action.

For more examples, take a look at these games in the Game Guide in Section 4 at the back of this book:

Band Aid Tag
Blob Tag
Sprout Ball
Giants, Wizards and Elves
One Fish Two Fish Red Fish Blue Fish

Two other activities that have a significant impact on the experience of competition are self-handicapping and taking turns. Although taking turns may be pretty self-explanatory, self-handicapping shows up in a lot of different ways, but perhaps most obviously in the reshuffling of teams. As in, "Jill and Susie, switch sides." Although this sounds straightforward, it is actually a fairly nuanced undertaking that requires kids to recognize that everyone's basic enjoyment of the experience is needed for the game to succeed. This, in turn, requires that students put the game's success ahead of their own. This concept of respecting the game is pretty radical, especially when considered in light of how we usually think about competition. At the heart of self-handicapping and respecting the game is the understanding and acceptance of our messy interdependence.

Small
Start:

Intentionally designing how teams are chosen also contributes significantly to students' ability to participate more joyfully and is in itself a powerful social norming process. By infusing arbitrariness in picking teams (e.g., having people with birthdays in January–June on one team and those with birthdays in July–December on the other), the social stigma of being picked last can be alleviated. Once a greater sense of rapport is established, pairing people by relative ability in any given sport and dividing teams in an explicit attempt to create fairness can be done in a way that is less hurtful and reinforces the message that what we value is a good game. The critical piece is in paying attention to how things feel and in emphasizing a collective end goal that values all participants. Navigating all of these demands gives students an extraordinary opportunity to develop strong relational abilities.

It may seem like a minor shift, but even just thinking about groupings instead of picking teams can make a big difference in the psychological impact of the experience. The **Whistle Mixer** activity is a great one for this. Just as you did in the Partner Challenge, you have students mingle in a defined space. The leader blows a whistle a given number of times and then students rush to get in groups of that number. Playing Whistle Mixer gets students used to getting into far more random groups—they are racing time and thinking less about who is in or out. Whistle Mixer can be played for multiple rounds, ending on the number of players you need for teams in the game to follow. In this way, Whistle Mixer can be a great transitional activity that sets you up with arbitrary groupings for whatever the next activity is, completely skipping over the potentially more loaded process of choosing sides.

Risky
Business

One of the things we commonly see when we arrive at a new school is that the existing "school rules" are almost exclusively focused on the physical nature of play. We've really seen it all—from no running to no playing tag, play segregated by age and gender, assigned games, and, more recently in COVID-19, social distancing guidance that includes preschoolers in chalk-drawn individual play zones.

And then there's Dodgeball. The prohibitions against Dodgeball are legion. Although this may be understandable, simply prohibiting the game has always seemed to me like giving up before you've even tried. And even if it is a controversial stance, at Playworks we believe that allowing kids to play Dodgeball—and to engage in other risky behaviors—should be the goal. A healthy version of the game reflects (and requires) a sense of agency and an understanding of interdependence. There may be risks involved, but students appreciate the respect inherent in allowing them to assume the responsibility for one another's safety. With the right setup,

Dodgeball becomes a practical way for them to experientially learn that the latitude to take risks is dependent on their ability to demonstrate the responsibility to handle it. Check out Sprout Ball in the Game Guide for more details on how to introduce the game safely.

Power of
Play:

Faced with the incredibly daunting task of keeping everyone safe, schools tend to focus on the physical as opposed to the emotional and social. Not unlike how we handle health more generally as a society, the actions we take to ensure safety are almost always reactive, as opposed to proactive or preventative. But learning requires risk-taking, so school safety programs need to be designed to enable physical and emotional risks and to ensure that safety isn't equated with the absence of risk, but rather with the development of skills and understanding that enable responsible risk-taking. School safety is an extraordinarily complex challenge to manage because of this inherent contradiction. Being safe requires students learn to manage risks, and learning to manage risks requires that students take risks.

Lenore Skenazy is a strong free-play advocate who has written and spoken extensively about the misapplication of safety. In 2008, Lenore wrote a column for the *New York Sun* entitled "Why I Let My 9-Year-Old Ride the Subway Alone," resulting in a flood of reaction and significant media coverage.[12] Looking at Lenore's decision from a completely rational perspective, allowing one's child to ride the subway or walk, as opposed to getting into a car and driving, is a significantly safer choice. Getting into a minivan with a parent is about the most dangerous thing kids do. Crime statistics make it clear that kids today are far safer than they were a generation ago, and that the public perception of crime and the reality don't match. We worry about the wrong things.

Lenore's new organization, Let Grow (founded with psychologist Peter Gray mentioned previously), works with teachers to incorporate activities designed to renormalize kids doing things on their own, thereby encouraging social-emotional learning through independence. The organization's signature activity, The Let Grow Project, encourages students to go home and do something new and outside their (and often their families') comfort zone, like riding their bike to the store, cooking on a stove or using a sharp knife, or going for a hike in the woods alone or with a friend. The students work with their families to negotiate and plan the activity and then complete it, reporting on the experience to the rest of the class. One of the things that Lenore describes as standing out in this process is the profound effect it has on parents. In relinquishing control and then witnessing their child's intrinsic abilities to analyze a situation, evaluate risk, and overcome obstacles, many parents describe the experience as transformational, as much, if not more, for themselves as for their children.

This is another important aspect of play: it helps us to make our comfort zones bigger. Fear is a real and valuable emotion. Like play, it has endured evolution because it helps us to survive. In order to not just survive, but to thrive, it is essential to learn to manage fear, and play helps us do that. Child psychologists working with toddlers have observed children turning to play in order to manage their fears, playing them out when they don't possess the language skills to express them verbally. For older children and adults, overcoming fear is often achieved through action. Play activities, such as climbing on the jungle gym or a game of hide and seek in which a child is simulating being in danger or lost, are inherently more low stakes and thus can be a critical tool in learning to manage the associated emotions.

BIG CHANGE #11

We learn to take Risks by Playing

Dealing with kids and their safety is a very real, and often defining, experience of running youth programs and schools. And in this Covid-moment, the stakes are extraordinarily high—not just for students, but for families and educators as well.

Early on in quarantine, the OSU professor I mentioned previously, Will Massey, described the different phases his family had already gone through—from the excitement at the initial novelty to moments of challenge. One noteworthy observation that Will made about his parenting experience during quarantine was his own tendency to invoke "safety" with his kids more out of convenience than actual concern. Yes, it was possible his daughter might hurt herself biking, but if he was honest with himself, the thing that was actually pushing him to restrict the behavior was the potential hassle of having to deal with something going wrong.

One of the key lessons from our work has been that prioritizing short-term convenience frequently undermines the longer-term benefits of supporting students' development of agency. Ensuring that students have the skills and understanding they need to determine the danger of a situation and to make informed and responsible decisions requires an upfront investment of time and energy. This is without doubt one of the most important investments of time that we can make. Especially as schools are reopening, engaging students in the co-creation of the rules and rituals that enable us to safely experiment with risk is essential to mitigating the anxieties that this moment may have prompted and the real threats that exist.

Small
Start:

As you might imagine, Playworks is a strong proponent of **Tag.** If you haven't played it in a while, you will be amazed by just how exhausting a good game of Tag can be. It's the original high-intensity interval training (HIIT). Tag is also one of the few games in which you can have a large group of youth constantly engaged at one time. In any case, to ensure that Tag can be safely and happily incorporated into the school day, we've come up with some solid Tag protocols, along with about a bazillion different Tag games.

The major Tag innovation that we promote is the sometimes mocked "Butterfly Fingers," which one achieves by wiggling ones fingers and committing to tagging one's fellow players only using a gentle butterfly-esque touch to the area of the shoulder, arms, or back. Scoff if you will, but Butterfly Fingers has won over even the most resistant of principals and by being silly with it, one can deescalate unwanted Tag intensity. Kids are going to fall down and scrape their knees, but that doesn't have to be exacerbated by an errant slap to the head in the process.

I've mentioned a couple of different tag games throughout the book. **Triangle Tag** involves four people with three holding hands and one, the tagger, standing outside. The players choose one of the three to be the runner and then the object is to move the triangle around in a way that prevents the tagger from reaching the runner. It's also a great way to practice the basketball skill of boxing out. When the tagger tags the runner, or the allotted time runs out, you switch places.

Wolves and Bunnies is another favorite and somewhat advanced team Tag game. To start, the leader needs to establish the boundaries and divide the participants into two groups—Wolves and Bunnies. The object is for the Wolves to tag all the Bunnies. The Bunnies can move all around as can the Wolves, except for the Wolf who has the ball (any ball will do). The Wolf in possession of the ball can only pivot and is the only Wolf who can tag Bunnies. When a Bunny is tagged, the player immediately turn into a Wolf. The team of Wolves works together, passing the ball quickly to one another, so as to tag nearby Bunnies. Play continues until there is only a small number of Bunnies left and they become the Wolves to kick off the next game.

It's a Family Affair

12

In March 2012 I was invited to Dublin, Ireland, along with 49 other social entrepreneurs to a three-day event called Change Nation. Hosted by Ashoka, the international fellowship for social entrepreneurs, the concept was to bring ideas to Ireland that had been effective in other countries, with the goal of adapting and adopting these solutions to meet the very real needs of a post–financial collapse Ireland. The three days were chock-full of meetings with Irish leaders from government, philanthropy, and citizen sector organizations, and as a result, it was agreed that Playworks would send staff members back to run a demonstration project in Dublin and Galway.

Ireland is a small country, and so the conversations around scaling—and the path to achieving country-wide change—felt very different from comparable discussions in the US. It's also a rapidly changing country, and in 2012, besides the economic challenges it faced, it was also a country wrestling with the collapse of its central organizing structure—the Catholic church—and a profound demographic shift, going from being a fairly homogenous population to an increasingly diverse one as the result of immigration and an Irish diaspora. It's also just a literally small country. The day I met with the Minister for Education, she smilingly noted that she'd heard I'd been at the pub with the O'Haras the night before.

In planning for the Ireland demonstration, we decided to send just two people—David Gallagher and the aforementioned coach, Tara Doherty. We also, importantly, made the decision that rather than trying to convince the Irish educators that they wanted Playworks to support recess for them there in Ireland, our goal was to convince them to let us train them to do it themselves. In this regard our trip to Ireland was an important experiment in not just training others, but in really turning over the reins. I have always been quick to point out that we didn't invent play, and that it is the original amateur activity. Nonetheless, it felt risky to have our name associated with programming that we really couldn't control. The only thing worse for kids than no recess, in our experience, is a bad recess.

The visit was well received. Tara still has a letter that was shared with her from a parent whose student had been particularly affected by the visit. The backstory was that the parents had been having concerns that their second-grade son, who had problems with his social skills, was not making friends at school. Prior to Playworks, they had come to observe *break,* the Irish word for recess, and had witnessed their son walking around by himself, not playing or interacting with anyone. The parents, obviously upset, had approached the school to share what they saw. The principal and teachers had been aware and were trying to take steps to address the situation, but had experienced little success.

The letter read:

> By chance I had arranged a meeting with Miss C. on Tuesday. She outlined details of the new American pilot scheme which commenced in yard. Having recently spoken to you regarding our son's difficulties in yard, I just wanted to share the positive things too! Normally he only talks about break time when something has upset him. I can safely say he has never told me about who he plays with or what games he has been involved in; it would truly be easier to get blood from a stone!!
>
> Having picked him up from school I was blown away, off his own back he started to talk about these "new games" he had played in yard. He sat down, drew pictures and explained the three games in great detail. He talked happily about them for over half an hour. Being aware that it is only a pilot scheme, I felt it was important to let you know the difference a day can make to a child, to see him happy as he skipped home from school, I cannot put it into words the positive effect!!

Power of
Play:

Being a parent is hard, but play can make it easier. We all have a lot of responsibilities and pressures, the world is an unsettling place, and, as parents, we find ourselves responsible for these, at least initially, small humans who are looking to us to help them make sense of the world around them. As previously described, playing with a child offers a whole new way to relate.

Play can also be an opportunity for families to support their students at school, broadening the triangle of school—student—family beyond academics and behavior to celebrating the development of young people together.

Our own experiences of school—whether we loved it or we never really fit in or something else—affect our ability and attitude about helping our kids navigate the experience for themselves. Compounding all this, schools vary dramatically in how they engage families. It's fair to say that many educators have (sometimes understandably, sometimes not) ambivalent feelings about parent involvement.

Having well-designed opportunities for families to meaningfully and appropriately engage in school-related activities can provide a critical opening. Parents and family members want and deserve the chance to support their students. It's not weird for them to want to be a part of their kids' education. It's also a developmental process. What's appropriate in preschool is different from what's good in elementary school and what's right in middle school and tolerable in high school. Play and sports can help with this developmental process by creating appropriate opportunities for parents to offer their love and support.

Nonetheless, sometimes trying to engage families can be challenging—and doing so when they are in the role of "sports fan" can feel a bit like a setup. All too often well-intentioned parents lose their perspective, cheering when the other team misses and just generally forgetting that the participants are nine- and 10-year-olds, often having their first-ever experience of competition. Inviting families to be part of creating an initial sporting experience for kids that is encouraging and incorporates a healthy attitude toward winning and losing can lead to a powerful "a-ha" moment for them.

Play is an Invitation to Families

One of the added benefits of offering sports leagues at Playworks has been that they also create a space for meaningful family engagement. Ensuring healthy participation requires planning and design, and to achieve this in our leagues we do two things in particular. First, before every game we huddle the two teams together—with players intentionally intermingled and families invited to listen in—and we review our goals for the evening's play. We actively involve the fans in this pregame ritual, reminding them and the players of our expectations—that they honor the game and cheer for both sides and always be positive. We ask that fans not yell coaching instructions from the sidelines, explaining that this could be particularly confusing for new players, especially when their guidance conflicts with what their coach has told them to do.

The second thing that helps shape the experience is that we invite family members to play, too. Whether it is a half-time shooting contest or a quick fan mini-game, inviting these adults to actually play together and in front of other people—to share the experience, to miss and to shine, to get winded running up and down the court, and to be momentarily confused about which basket is theirs— dramatically shifts the nature of the cheering. Done with kindness and a bit of humor, all the things we know about play take effect almost immediately, tapping their empathy and lightening the mood.

When adults support kids in healthy and positive competition, we open so many doors for them and us. We support their development of new skills, we offer a nurturing reminder that winning and losing aren't the only points of the game, and we bear witness to the joy of play.

Small
Start:

A great way to introduce any sport is through a **Three Lines** version of the game, broken down to emphasize one or two particular skills. This can be done with soccer, hockey, or football. An all-time favorite, and one we've had a lot of fun introducing Playworks families to, is **Three Lines Basketball.** The setup for Three Lines is pretty straightforward. You just need three cones spaced out evenly across the court at roughly the centerline facing toward a basket. Ask the players to line up behind the three cones evenly and then it helps to start by reviewing the rule that you're focusing on for the day. This might involve demonstrating how to dribble with one hand, explaining traveling (taking more than two steps without dribbling), passing techniques (bounce and chest passes), or how to defend another player without making contact (shuffling their feet with arms up or wide).

Invite the first three players of each line to step into the court to play the first round of defense against the next three players. The teams play a quick game of three-on-three with each team trying to score first. You can modify the play to focus on a particular skill by creating rules like no dribbling—only passing—or that each player on a team must touch the ball a certain number of times before shooting. The team that scores stays on as defense playing against the next group of three, with the team of three that didn't score returning to the end of the lines. If a team doesn't score in the allotted time—no more than a minute—then the leader encourages all the line standers to count down from ten. If no one has scored at the end of the time, then both teams leave the court and two new teams start. If a team wins three times in a row, it gets a celebratory clap and returns to the end of the line as well.

Let's Get
Physical

13

When Kyle DeRoos was growing up in Sheboygan, Wisconsin, playing sports was a serious thing. He went to a small school, so pretty much everyone got to play who wanted to, but he got the message that when it came to sports, the idea was to be good at it. Not in a worrisome way, just in an "of course, that's how it is" kind of way. So it came as something of a surprise when he started working as a Sports4Kids coach, and he found himself in a job where the whole point seemed to be finding joy in doing something you're not good at. There was no pressure, and he realized that more than anything else, his job was to create opportunities for kids to find their place in the activities he was running. The sports and games were secondary to the experience that the kids were having, and he realized that the most important thing wasn't to be good at sports, it was to have the sports be good for kids.

Power of
Play:

It's commonly recognized that play can increase physical health and aide in curbing obesity, but it connects to the issue as a significantly upstream approach. When kids have access to daily play, they are more likely to engage in vigorous physical activity, which may ultimately be the single biggest determinant of overall well-being—physical and mental. In this way, it does make sense to hold up play as a tool for combatting inactivity. It may be obvious, but obesity and physical inactivity are not the same things, and contrary to our cultural biases, being inactive is a greater health risk than being overweight. A study reported in 2015 in the *American Journal of Clinical Nutrition* found that being inactive could be twice as dangerous as carrying too much weight.[13]

Although working to minimize obesity is an important pursuit, many of our attitudes about obesity are discriminatory. Many people hold strong biases against those who are heavier, and these attitudes can be profoundly damaging to women and girls, in particular. Furthermore, the cultural, economic, and political factors involved in obesity are often overlooked, negatively affecting our efforts to address it as a health issue. Even if play is not a direct strategy for managing obesity in children, it is an important activity to prioritize in ensuring that the environment supports a physically and emotionally healthy lifestyle, which is associated with a healthy weight. Play alone cannot mitigate the challenges that stem from inequitable access to healthy foods, green spaces, and affordable health care, but access to daily play can still contribute to students developing healthy habits.

* * *

Dr. John Ratey, an associate clinical professor of psychiatry at Harvard Medical School, wrote a book called *Spark: The Revolutionary New Science of Exercise and the Brain* in 2008 that opens with the story of Naperville Central High School, just outside Chicago.[14] The gym teachers in Naperville conducted an experiment they called Zero Hour P.E., in which the students basically worked out before school. The focus was on running and other exercises in which you are competing against yourself to improve—as opposed to competitive team sports. The results, as Ratey describes, were notable. Not only did Naperville students become the "fittest" in the nation, the experiment showed significant academic improvement among the students as well. Dr. Ratey explained these results as the natural outcome of exercise's beneficial brain chemistry:

> *Exercise increases the concentration of both dopamine and norepinephrine, as well as other brain chemicals. I have always said that a dose of exercise is like taking a bit of Ritalin or Adderall. It's similar to taking a stimulant. Second, over time, exercise helps build up the machinery to increase the amount of neurotransmitters in the brain as well as their postsynaptic receptors. Chronic exercise eventually causes growth of the system. The more fit that you are, the better the system works.*

Although the benefits of the Zero Hour P.E. program were remarkable, as someone who loves to exercise and is also the mother of a blended family of five kids, my honest reaction to the Naperville experiment was something in between "of course" and "no way." My kids have all participated on teams, played in a ton of pick-up games, and have even taken up recreational running for varying lengths of time. One of my kids could legitimately be described as something of a morning person. But getting my kids to school on time has been a challenge since they were in preschool, and the idea of getting them to school for a Zero Hour P.E. so that they could exercise before school feels like it would be a Herculean endeavor. And this points to the larger challenge with PE in general: although it is hugely beneficial, making time for exercise at school is often unpopular. Between student resistance and academic pressures on time, the struggle is real. Adding in budgetary constraints makes it almost impossible.

At a conference a few years back, I was on a panel with some physical education leaders who were talking about the challenges of meeting the federal guideline that children and adolescents get an hour of daily physical activity. Before I thought better of it, I blurted out, "It may be hard to get kids to exercise for an hour, but it's super simple to get them to play for an hour."

As defined by the CDC, *physical education* "provides cognitive content and instruction designed to develop motor skills, knowledge, and behaviors for physical activity and physical fitness."[15] Physical education has always been a combination of doing and studying, and in this way it is more aligned with kinesiology, the science behind exercise, physical movement, and sports. Since the early 2000s, PE minutes have been decreasing as a result of heightened academic and budgetary pressures. An increasingly common practice in elementary schools is to ask classroom teachers to take responsibility for leading physical education, even though most teaching preparation programs don't offer any significant instruction in this area.

In California, there is an unfunded state mandate of 200 minutes of PE for every 10 days of elementary instruction and 400 minutes for every 10 days for middle and high schoolers. In practice it works out to be much less than this. A policy brief from the Active Living Research Group reviewed a statewide study in which 82 percent of fifth graders studied attended schools in districts that failed to provide the mandated minimum level of PE, with Latinx and African American fifth graders, along with those eligible for free and reduced lunch, disproportionately more likely to attend schools in noncompliant districts.[16]

Although it's easy to point to these numbers as a clear example of inequity, figuring out the root of the problem is a little more complicated. Without a more equitable distribution of school funding, asking school leaders to prioritize physical education when they are being held accountable to significant academic measures is basically a nonstarter. Compounding the issues of time and staffing constraints, the ugly truths about the state of our school facilities, safety concerns, and a socially accepted dismissal of PE's importance, create an uphill battle at best.

The difference in the experience between choosing to exercise and being forced to exercise—as anyone who has ever made a new year's resolution can attest—is significant. If one of the goals of promoting play in schools is to offer additional physical activity, the key to achieving this goal is to focus first and foremost on creating an inclusive environment that provides multiple points of entry for participation and emphasizes student choice and voice. This is more likely to happen at recess when students are motivated intrinsically to participate, rather than through a class that has goals and measures over which students have no influence. Although PE is critical to students' understanding of a healthy lifestyle and their knowledge about fitness and nutrition, it is essential that PE and recess be paired and prioritized equally to ensure that students have the broad range of experiences that promote a lifetime of physical activity.

In order to engage kids in even moderate physical activity through play, a foundation that attends to students' sense of safety and belonging is needed. It is all part of a virtuous cycle that requires intentional design and ongoing nurturing that centers students' intrinsic motivation and agency. Once the conditions for play are met, the physical benefits are many.

Play gets us Moving

An aspect of play and physicality that deserves mention is the importance of learning to be aware of, and responsive to, the messages our bodies send us. In this extraordinarily distracted age, it is easy to spend a significant part of our waking hours anywhere but in the present.

We have talked about the connections among play and emotions, agency, and mitigating risk. All of these elements have attendant physical manifestations that we can learn to manage through play. Whether it is the feeling in the pit of one's stomach when experiencing fear, an ache in the chest when one feels hurt, the lift in one's shoulders that can accompany a burst of confidence, the full-bodied tightness of anger or the sweaty palms of nervousness, our emotions and our thoughts are inextricably intertwined with our bodies. There is also a physical feeling associated with compassion—whether one is feeling it toward oneself or others—that play creates opportunities to practice.

Schools can often exacerbate this compartmentalization of mind and body, treating student bodies as vehicles responsible for getting their heads from place to place. But we learn with our bodies. Embodied cognition is the idea that what happens in our minds arises from our actions and interactions with the world around us. Lessons taught without being grounded in experiential opportunities to explore and physically make sense of that knowledge make it harder for students to understand and remember the information that is being conveyed. And this is true whether we are talking about math and history or social and emotional learning.

Schools are the place where young humans learn many of their coping skills when it comes to managing the mind-heart-body connection. Encouraging students to be in their bodies—mindfully—and to listen to their bodies should be an essential aspect of educating children and one that is achieved through access to healthy play.

Respecting and supporting young people—even our youngest students—to interpret the messages they are getting from their own bodies about what they need, what feels safe for them, what feels right and wrong, and how to manage those feelings can make a significant difference in their ability to learn and in their ability to trust themselves and others. Much more impactful than just looking at weight loss or releasing energy, play affects the larger human ecosystem in a way that not only supports the individual's mind-body connection but also reinforces positive interactions among individuals and groups that power a complex system of interdependence.

Small
Start:

One of the big challenges of running games for large groups of kids is that their needs can be contradictory. For example, sometimes you really just need to run around, and sometimes you want to take it slow. To address this, we've found it helpful to create "Ultimate" variations on more standard games that make room for many different physical ways of being in the game—at the same time. A great example of this is **Ultimate Kickball.** For purposes of this explanation I'm going to assume that you have at least a vague familiarity with kickball—it's essentially baseball with a big red rubber ball and you use your foot instead of bat. In Ultimate Kickball you start just like in regular kickball, dividing the group into two teams, a kicking team and a fielding team. The pitcher controls the play of the game and play begins when the ball is rolled to the kicker and stops when the pitcher has the ball. The kicker kicks the ball and runs the bases in order, earning one point for each runner that rounds all bases and reaches home base safely. Runners cannot continue running the bases if their fly ball is caught before it bounces or if they are tagged while not on a base.

But that's where the similarities stop. In Ultimate Kickball, there are no foul balls and players can kick the ball backwards if there is a backstop or wall behind home plate. Also, there can be more than one runner on a base at any time, with runners choosing to stay on one base if they think it's unsafe to run. Runners can pass each other at any time, but they must return to the previous base if the pitcher has the ball before they are halfway to the next base. Teams switch after everyone on the kicking team has kicked once.

Paradoxically, by stretching the rules to allow a range of different behaviors, the ultimate versions of games enable more players of different levels to find their best and most fun way to participate.

Time-Out:
What We
Measure Matters

Back in 2003, California Volunteers was making a coordinated effort to address the nation's obesity crisis, and we were encouraged to apply as a part of this focus. California Volunteers is the body that coordinates the state's grants for AmeriCorps, the national service program that was initially conceived under the first former president Bush and then launched in earnest by former president Clinton. AmeriCorps has created important service opportunities for people, especially young adults, and provides significant support to nonprofit organizations and schools in particular.

Taking money to do something that you're not really committed to is an ever-present danger for nonprofit organizations and generally a really bad idea. When we started working with AmeriCorps, we were completely forthcoming with our program officer that we didn't see ourselves as an anti-obesity program. We were comfortable in our role in increasing physical activity, but we recognized that we had extremely limited influence over what our students were eating or other conditions in their lives and were thus unlikely to influence obesity as a stand-alone initiative. Our program officer assured us that it was all good—that he understood what we did and who we were and that we were exactly the kind of out-of-the-box approach to addressing physical inactivity that they believed essential to addressing the obesity crisis. And then he took another job.

Our new program officer was a strong proponent of project management through data, and she insisted that the delivery of our program be accompanied by three separate weight and BMI (body mass index) measures throughout the year of all of the students in our California schools. To make this happen, we asked researchers from UC Berkeley to develop a legitimate process. We bought BMI scales. We trained our staff to run students through a series of games and activities that involved taking off their shoes, jumping on and off scales, and lying down next to a tape measure on the ground. Relying on the universal American ignorance about the metric system, we did our measurements in kilos and centimeters in an effort to minimize any stigma. We brought an insane amount of playfulness and creativity to the process, but there was no escaping that the whole thing was a bit of a dumpster fire.

Perhaps the worst moment that I remember was being out at a school where we had just finished running our fifth class of 30 kids through the process. The coach at that school, a young woman named Summer, asked me a question that was clearly troubling her: "Is this why we're doing it?" Her question cut right to the heart of the matter. If we were putting all this effort into measuring kids' weight, did that mean it was the reason Playworks existed?

I have no idea what I actually said to Summer that day. I remember feeling exhausted and I probably also felt angry and foolish. I'm sure I wanted to answer honestly with the full force of my frustration, but I was also compelled to not let Summer feel like she was totally wasting her time. I undoubtedly babbled something vague and noncommittal and probably mildly incomprehensible. Although this certainly wasn't the only time I mismanaged a situation—nor, for that matter, the only time we took anti-obesity money—it was the time I remember most clearly feeling like I had let down our staff. This was the moment in which I really came to understand the extent to which "we are what we measure."

We don't often consider the extent to which data collection has a profound impact on how we spend our time and thus what we are thinking about. Inevitably these activities shape who we are and what we believe, as individuals and as organizations. We realized that in having staff members spend so much time focused on measuring kids' weight we were sending a very direct message about what they should be focused on and what they should care about, when that wasn't what we actually intended. Measurement is a significant sign of what we value. Recognizing this and committing to measure the things we care most about is critical for building organizations and school cultures where our values are reinforced by our actions.

Here, There, and Everywhere

14

Over the years, Playworks has run recess in almost every conceivable setting—from rooftop playgrounds in San Francisco and New York City to schoolyards where portable classrooms have been "temporarily" plopped in the middle; from tiny urban concrete playgrounds to massive pastures; and from hot desert-baked playgrounds in Phoenix to the frozen tundra of Minnesota playgrounds in February. (Pro tip: powdered Kool-Aid can be used to draw out non-toxic Four Square courts on a snow-covered blacktop!) And while we're not saying it is always easy, play is still always possible.

We have played in the rain, snow, and haboobs (intense dust storms that happen in the desert, including Arizona, and sometimes they mix with rain, which means that you have mud flying through the air, and, I admit, we moved the play inside when the haboob hit). We have played in cafetoriums, designed games that can be played at a desk, and, more recently, played virtually. One of the many amazing things about play is that it is inherently adaptive—not just to the skills and abilities of the participants, but also to the space and equipment that you have available. All that is really required is some imagination and a willingness to flex.

Back in 2005 after Hurricane Katrina, our staff members began asking what we might do to help. We ended up arranging for teams of coaches to travel to Houston where they were housed by local residents, and where they were able to provide activities at the Astrodome and at local schools where kids from areas affected by Katrina had been relocated. The experience of organizing these trips proved inspiring for all of us, and our California school partners were supportive. One of the most memorable things from this time was the way the Junior Coaches in California stepped up to keep recess running smoothly while their coaches were away helping in Houston. I remember one little girl explaining to me that it made her feel like she was helping the kids from New Orleans, too.

Our time in Houston was a powerful reminder that people can literally play anywhere, and that, especially when the context of a given space is challenging, play is all that much more important. Our staff members led hours of daily games in the Astrodome parking lot, providing the kids with a much-needed reminder of normalcy and their families a much-needed moment to breathe. As you might imagine, the parking lot was a massive expanse of pavement with lots of vehicles coming and going to deliver food and other supplies. Our coaches made the space—and the transitions to and from the space—work by cordoning off a play area with cones and by creating a ritual around gathering in the stadium and then jogging out (accompanied by cheering adult supporters) like one of the professional Houston sports teams. In a difficult situation, play served to help mitigate the space's limitations and maximize its assets through ritual and design.

Power of
Play:

Although physical space is often brought up as an obstacle to making play accessible, we've also seen that spaces are local and cultural and that the context associated with different locales can have a significant impact on what is possible and how the environment feels. Are there geographic considerations, such as weather? What about social issues that are unique to the area?

Oftentimes challenges that are masquerading as space constraints are really human conflicts in disguise. From the emotionally charged experience of schools merging to the politically fraught dynamics of charter schools renting out space from a mainstream public school with declining enrollment, sharing is hard, and change that we do not choose is scary. These impacts on space have just as much influence as the location of the basketball court. Starting with mapping the yard will help (see the Small Start), but incorporating other levers such as roles and rituals can make a big difference in managing the many ways that context affects space.

Play can happen Anywhere

Play can be adapted to work in any space, and it's important to recognize how the space you have available aligns with your goals and to be intentional in determining how you use and shift your space to best meet your needs. Right now we have a new opportunity to redesign how space is used for play in schools. Considering how we might reimagine the experience of school, integrating new understandings and being open to new ways of moving forward is critical to centering student well-being.

When thinking about different spaces, recognizing their inherent strengths and challenges can be the starting point for designing optimal experiences for students. Whether that is indoors or outdoors, online or in person, playing with these spaces represents an opportunity to maximize resources and exemplifies the importance of adaptation and flexibility in problem-solving and life.

The 21st century has shown us that space need not be limited to a physical location—a lesson that the 2020 COVID-19 pandemic in particular has really driven home. It's probably fair to say that Playworks resisted going online initially, in no small part because we had always seen ourselves—and in-person play more generally—as the antidote to a culture that was moving pell-mell toward becoming increasingly virtual and disconnected. But in 2017–2018, we made a significant investment in developing an online platform that playfully invited people to join us in the movement of making safe and healthy play available daily to all kids. RecesssLab.org was built to encourage educators—along with administrators and concerned family members—across the country to assess their own recess and to have a place where they could get information about how to make recess better. We wanted to make sure people had access to useful tools that would help them individually and that also playfully deputized them as advocates for play in their communities.

Developing RecessLab.org coincided with our work with Professor Will Massey, the Oregon State professor referenced previously, and we were able to include a lighter version of the validated recess assessment tool in the form of a Recess Checkup. We widely promoted the website and tool—with some significant support from partners such as Action for Healthy Kids and Alliance for a Healthier Generation—and to both our delight and surprise, thousands of people signed up and took the checkup. The results were sobering, with the vast majority of schools coming nowhere close to what we had established as the bar for safe and healthy play. And we were struck by the thousands of teachers who responded to the optional request for comments with their concerns about the absence of daily healthy play and the overall state of recess at their schools. Our initial foray into the digital space made it clear that there was a need and demand for services in this area.

Our learning in establishing RecessLab.org inspired us to believe that adult engagement digitally in play was possible and further that it would enable us to extend our reach in a way that was cost-effective and thus more accessible. This was the genesis of PlayworksU, our digital training platform. PlayworksU is focused on educators and emphasizes play-based activities that start in the classroom. Although we had initially conceived of PlayworksU as a tool to attract and serve new schools, we found that schools where we already had in-person programs were also interested in adopting it. One of the most common use cases we saw was a school staff collectively watching (and playing along with) one of the PlayworksU three-minute lessons to kick off its staff meetings.

When COVID-19 hit in March 2020, we already had a digital presence, and although not at all ready for the kind of pivot the pandemic would require, we felt way more prepared than we might have. We had experience building virtual content and an instructional designer on staff, but doing *everything* remotely was a new challenge. That spring our staff, largely representing the generation of digital natives, leaned in to live, daily recess shared on Facebook, which we made available for free to thousands of households.

Once we were able to navigate the challenges of remote coordination, adapting recess for the online experience was actually far more straightforward than we had initially anticipated. Our coaches selected games that worked for small groups or for even just one child to play and filmed themselves providing instructions just as they would if they were on the playground. Modifications that made it less likely to break something—like using torn paper in lieu of a ball for a catching and counting exercise or moving around the room with little tiny fast steps (aka fire feet) made it possible for most kids to participate in almost any space. When we began to work more closely with schools in fall 2020, incorporating recess into the classroom Zoom setup, the interaction with students made even more variations of games possible. All in all, the quick pandemic shift to online recess was an extraordinary tribute to play's inherent ability to adapt to whatever physical constraints arise.

Small
Start:

Mapping the Yard is a pretty straightforward exercise that can have surprising results because it compels us to thoughtfully consider things that are right in front of us but are still often overlooked. The exercise begins, as you might imagine, by taking a blank piece of paper and drawing out the schoolyard—or the space you use for play—as it currently exists. Right from the start, people's hesitancy about communicating visually is often an issue. I want to reassure you, and whomever you are doing this exercise with, that your maps don't have to look perfect—or even good for that matter. Providing pencils, rulers, and working erasers can help. Once an outline of the space is created, make at least one copy to save for later.

Using one of the copies, the goal is to indicate the patterns of activity that exist in your space on the map. We recommend using colored pencils or crayons and making notes indicating where, what, when, and how kids and adults use the space. Is there Four

Square? A basketball court? Do kids play different games on the basketball courts during different periods? Are there pinch points impinging on the flow of students—coming out of the cafeteria doors, for example—or dead zones where nothing ever happens? Note if there are areas of concern—places on the playground that aren't easily visible or where the ball frequently gets kicked over a fence or onto a roof. The idea is to get as much detail as possible onto the map to help see what's really happening and to inspire ideas in response to what works and what doesn't.

After these descriptions of what's happening have been created, take the copy of the blank outline and imagine the range and flow of activities you'd *like* to see. Sometimes it helps to have multiple copies of the blank outline and to offer up different scenarios, such as design a schoolyard if money were no object or if it were always sunny. It's even worthwhile to design the worst possible schoolyard, if only to call out the attributes that you really, really want to avoid.

We start this mapping process out individually—our staff members usually do it on their own—and then invite others to join, grown-ups and kids. One way to ease people into the experience is to share your blank outline of the existing outside space as a collective jumping off place. We've found that when school staff members share their interpretations of the current state of things and offer their ideas for improving the schoolyard, it can be a revelatory experience in the ways that their perceptions differ but also in the insight that nothing about these patterns of use has to be permanent.

Once you have mapped your space, you can more intentionally explore the potential for play and design the way people move through, behave in, and engage with the areas you have to use.

Bringing just a little bit of structure to this aspect of how students interact on the playground and using the environment to create cues for expectations makes it much easier to give students a greater degree of control over the actual play experience. Signage that explains the process for borrowing and sharing equipment, markings on the ground for Four Square that include a place for students to line up, and cones set up to create visual reminders of the boundaries for different games all ultimately contribute to students having far more agency over the actual play and more time to do so.

Chaos
by Design

15

I have often joked that when it comes to Playworks' impact, I am happy to take credit for anything good that has happened within a five-mile radius. Nevertheless, I was surprised when a principal reached out to let me know that she was convinced that our program was having an impact because there was no longer graffiti in the school bathroom. I asked for clarification, and she explained that prior to the advent of Playworks, the boys at her school had been so bored and disgruntled at recess that they had taken to sneaking into the bathroom and tagging the walls when they were supposed to be out on the playground. She had assigned a male teacher to "guard" the bathroom during recess, and that had had some effect, but the teacher found the assignment tedious and onerous and when called away, the behavior would immediately resume.

So much about this story feels emblematic of how we get education wrong, even when our intentions are for the best. Whether it is
testing, standardized curriculum, or silent passing in the hallways
(the practice of compelling students to be completely quiet
and lined up single file while transitioning from the classroom to
lunch or out to recess), ideas that come from a place of good intention can have huge unintended consequences if designed as
reactions to a bad situation, rather than being proactively imagined
to advance teaching and learning. Assigning a teacher to watch the
bathroom instead of making the effort to understand why the boys
were in the bathroom tagging in the first place—recess was
boring—led to a particularly inefficient and generally unsatisfying
use of a limited resource (the teacher's time). Had the principal
designed for the root cause, she could have assigned the teacher to
be outside making recess fun, benefiting everyone and
contributing more significantly to the overall school climate.

Power of
Play:

Play is a design lever that can be intentionally employed to build
trust in a group, spark creativity, or even to create a less serious vibe
in an effort to encourage greater comfort with making mistakes.
Over the years we've noticed that in designing great play activities,
it's critical to also consider the other design levers (the aspects of a
given experience that you can intentionally manipulate to qualita-
tively change how a participant feels). Throughout the book we've

explored a number of these: in looking at Junior Coaches and adults we've considered roles; in bringing in games and describing our leagues we've delved into rituals; and, in thinking about mapping the yard, we considered space. Exploring how all these different design levers interact, along with their respective strengths and challenges, is critical to creating memorable and innovative experiences.

Group management challenges are by far the most frequent reason that Playworks is invited to partner with a school. Looking at these as design challenges, as opposed to intractable problems, is the key to how we try and support schools in addressing them. We find it helps to believe that if you have a problem related to managing kids, play can help you solve it.

Using the human-centered design framework, we start with empathy. Interviewing the people involved—students, teachers, cafeteria workers, and bus drivers—can offer insights that help you make sure you're solving for the right problem. Turning these interviews into a playful learning experience can be a great way to begin the process of shifting challenging behaviors. Involving students creates an opening for them to not only be a part of addressing the dynamic but also invites them to assume responsibility. Encouraging students to consider playful solutions—for example, designing a ritual for the start of an afterschool program to help students arrive on time and effectively transition from the school day—can also tap their intrinsic motivation to be a part of the desired change.

It's also worth noting that the design levers that influence how group experiences feel start with the invitation to participate and continue long after it's over—through the stories that are told and the other ways that the experience is debriefed. In other words, even in-person spaces have a virtual element to them in our imaginations and memories, and designing those aspects of the experience matters almost as much as the activity itself. Bringing a playful lens to intentionally engaging with all the different elements of experience design can dramatically increase participants' sense of belonging.

Play helps us create the best possible Experiences for Kids

Intentional design on the playground shows up in the rituals, roles, and physical layout of the outdoor space. When students come out to recess and find the yard set up with cones that indicate suggested games and boundaries, along with the equipment needed and even signage that ensures that there is a shared understanding of the rules and expectations, they are set up for success in quickly jumping into an activity and maximizing their limited recess time.

When there are Junior Coaches (ours wear bright purple t-shirts to identify them) who are freely disbursing High Fives and encouraging words to younger students and peers trying a new activity, they serve to reinforce expectations for inclusion and treating one another with kindness. For younger students, they see this role taking responsibility for one's peers and one's school as one to which they can aspire.

When there are predictable rituals that mark the process of transitioning in and out of class for recess, for celebrating a great effort and for shaking off a mistake, the intentional design of play is being brought into service of the larger goals of helping students build the skills that enable taking risks, making mistakes, and navigating change.

Small Start:

Tell Me My Story is a storytelling exercise that has no apparent purpose, and yet it consistently creates an experience for participants that compels them to better understand themselves and their partners. The activity works by breaking people into pairs and asking that each pair identify a Partner A and Partner B. Partner A is then asked to tell Partner B a three-minute story of a time when he or she was succeeding wildly, or "crushing it," with as much detail as possible. Partner B listens without asking any questions. At the end of the story a quick debrief will often elicit comments about how people found it difficult to tell a story about their own success, or others will say how much they enjoyed being reminded of the memory.

After this debrief, Partner B is then asked to tell Partner A the story he or she just heard, but in the first person. In other words, Partner B is to tell Partner A Partner A's story as if it had happened to Partner B. After some nervous giggles, it is fascinating to watch people lean in to the activity. People will describe the retelling as stressful—they didn't want to get the other person's story wrong—or anxiety-producing because they worry they weren't listening as closely as they should have been. But almost invariably, the listeners find the experience of having their own story told back to them moving. They hear it differently, feel more seen, or are struck by the complimentary details that the retelling has added. Not infrequently, the retelling of the story actually comes *closer* to the essential truths. The second part of the exercise is a reversal of roles and although the element of surprise is lost, the experiences are often very similar.

Ch-Ch-Ch-
Changes

16

My go-to story on the power of transitions—on the importance of successfully and intentionally navigating moments of change—is from the early days of Sports4Kids when Justin Robinson, a coach who went by JRo, was assigned to work at Seneca Center. The Seneca Center Family of Agencies runs a number of different programs focused on unconditional care, and Playworks' earliest partnership with them involved placing one of our coaches at a school they ran for students with severe emotional disabilities. JRo was our first staffer placed there, and he had to go through our training on leading games and building community, as well as Seneca's staff training, which prepared him for the more specific demands of its population.

It was at an early Sports4Kids staff training that JRo shared everything he was learning about the importance of communication in effectively managing transitions, especially for students who had severe emotional disabilities. JRo explained that Seneca would let the students know when a transition was coming and then explain it in detail so that everyone involved knew exactly what to expect. They would check in while the transition was happening, reminding the students where they were in the process, and then they would debrief the transition once it was completed.

Although it sounded like a lot of extra effort, our staff members immediately latched on to the importance of this level of care in ensuring that everyone felt safe and able to make it work. They understood that this was what it took to set everyone up for success and that the upside of spending time doing it this way far outstripped the downside of the hassle. Also, we quickly learned that by creating playful rituals to mark the transition and by turning over the management of these rituals to the students, we could basically transform the whole thing into a game.

Power of
Play:

William Bridges wrote a book in the 1970s called *Transitions* that dug deeply into the power of change in our lives.[17] He explained that every transition is essentially made up of three parts—an ending, a messy middle, and a new beginning—and that humans tend to have certain patterns in dealing with these moments of passage. For example, if you start dating someone new before fully breaking up with your last partner, skipping over the feelings about your breakup and jumping right into a new relationship, that behavior is likely to show up in how you end jobs and even how you exit parties. Being aware of how one handles transitions, and then making a concerted effort to fully experience each phase in turn, Bridges argues, is the key to happily navigating change. Years of leading play activities in schools has confirmed this understanding and heightened our awareness that transitions are where things are most likely going to break down, especially when students and adults are experiencing added stress. Taking the time to thoroughly end an activity, calling attention to the transition, and then gathering before launching into the new activity can make all the difference in the world.

Play makes Transitions way better for Everyone

Transitions show up throughout the play experience, and our ability to support students in making them gracefully has been key to our success in convincing school staff that the investment of time in play is worthwhile. Beyond the transitions from the classroom out to recess and back again, play can be effectively incorporated into transitions at the beginning and end of the school day and during the day when shifting activities in the classroom. Greeting students at the doorway in the mornings with an individualized handshake can contribute to a welcoming environment that reinforces students' sense that they are seen and valued members of a community. Establishing playful rituals about how a class shifts from one activity to the next can lessen anxieties by creating a degree of predictability that increases students' sense of control over the world around them.

At Playworks we work actively to train our staff members in using a lot of different facilitation tools, emphasizing the importance of finding the tools with which they feel most comfortable and infusing play whenever possible. The Group Agreements that we talked about in Big Change 8 are always a good place to start with any facilitated effort—especially calling out a value that might be particularly relevant to an upcoming activity. There are books and books about becoming a skilled facilitator, but here are some of the more play-important facilitation tools and activities we frequently use, very briefly described:

Think/Pair/Share. In Think, Pair, Share, students are invited to engage with a challenge first on their own (the Think mode), then in discussion with a partner (Pair), and then in the larger group (Share). For students who find big-group discussions intimidating, this framework can help make participation a little more manageable.

Stacking. A teacher or group leader makes note of the people who have raised their hand and announces the order in which they will be called. This helps lessen students' worry about not getting their turn and encourages students to listen to others while they are waiting. We encourage staff members to keep track of who raises their hand and whom they call on to watch for student hesitancy in participation and their own unconscious bias.

Validating. When a student expresses anger or frustration—or really, when they express any feeling or emotion—we encourage staff members to validate the feelings expressed. This does not necessarily mean that you agree with the content of what the child is saying, only that you are acknowledging him or her, which is often enough to help a student stay engaged.

Proximity. When students are getting off task or engaged in side talk, simply moving closer to them as you continue to facilitate can be more effective than breaking your flow to call out their behavior.

The Whip-Around. This is a structured go-around that encourages everyone to weigh in. This can be used as a wrap up activity or as a bounce back when one of the participants asks a particularly interesting or challenging question.

ORID. ORID stands for objective, reflective, interpretive, and decisional—which may sound kind of extra for recess, but we use it mostly for trainings with adults and with questions such as these: What did you see and hear? How did you feel? Why did we play these games? How will you use these games in your program? How have I been getting your attention throughout the training?

Small
Start:

Like any workplace, Playworks has its share of meetings. Whether in-person or remotely, people show up at these meetings in a wide variety of states. In order to get everyone reconnected—and to help manage the transition from doing whatever they were doing to actually being present—we start off every meeting with a quick and preferably light-hearted **Check-in Question.** These can be apropos of nothing—"What was your first concert?" "If you had to/got to live in another country for a year, which country would you choose?"—or they can be relevant to a certain moment in time or event— "Favorite Thanksgiving food?" "Best birthday ever?" The point is to invite people to acknowledge that we are all three-dimensional humans who come to work in the context of our lives and the world around us. You must be present to win!

Driven to Distraction

17

JG Larochette started his career as a Playworks coach, and left after a couple of years to try and bring the joy and fun from the playground to the classroom as a teacher. Although he was passionate about supporting students, in his eight years of being a teacher he experienced schools and classrooms as poorly equipped to support the mental and emotional well-being of students and staff. Although JG was able to build on his experience as a Playworks coach, infusing fun into his teaching, he nonetheless started experiencing greater levels of anxiety seeing the daily stress and trauma in the lives of his students. Depression set in, and JG turned to yoga and therapy, which helped, but it was mindfulness that ultimately enabled him to regain his sense of purpose. JG began to experiment with introducing mindfulness to his students and realized immediately that it made a huge difference. He also recognized that he needed to make sure that the experience was culturally relevant for the students at his school. In fall 2012, building on all that he had learned, JG founded Mindful Life Project, a nonprofit that empowers underserved students through mindfulness training, yoga, and hip-hop in Richmond, California.

Power of
Play:

Playworks' adaptation to the online space has compelled me to reconsider the nature of our collective distraction. Rather than reducing it to simply having our attention consumed by all things virtual, it has become increasingly clear that the issue is more accurately characterized by our collective inability to maintain focus for extended periods of time. Our experiences with play suggest that this can be achieved in-person and in more distributed states, but that it requires an intentional effort to create environments that emphasize the importance of participants being able to really see and connect with others and to have the experience of being truly seen themselves.

The state of play is also one that allows for our brains to quiet down. In the first Big Change when I described the Small Start "I Love My Neighbor," I mentioned that I like playing an adult version, "Stand Up," when speaking to groups of adults. One of the biggest realizations that participants take away from this game is the recognition that moments when we are playing represent a potential respite from the steady stream of thoughts and lists and worries and feelings that our brains are constantly churning out.

Play is also a powerful tool for refocusing a group when distraction sets in. Using play to create a break in the action and reorient to the purpose at hand can make it easier to get back on track. Along these same lines, going outside has a similar power to help our brains quiet down and to counteract distraction. The combination of play and being outside may be one of the most magical forces for good, one that is too often forgotten or overlooked as a tool in helping our students develop the power of concentration.

Achieving this state of profound focus—what Mihaly Csikszentmihalyi dubbed the "flow state"—requires an unlikely combination of vulnerability and independence.[18] This state of complete absorption is characterized by a merging of action and awareness, an amplified sense of agency, and a loss of self-consciousness. It can be so engrossing that other needs are forgotten, and there is a sense of freedom from time. It also sounds decidedly like the definition of *play*. Creating opportunities for students to experience flow like this is essential to helping them understand all that they are capable of.

We are more Present when we Play

It's worth noting here that seeking distraction can be an understandable reaction to a hectic world, and that a child going out to recess who simply wants to space out for a few minutes between scheduled activities is well within his or her rights. Leveraging play to promote focus is particularly valuable because it requires student volition. Students are choosing to focus and to be present in the game, and that fundamentally changes the experience.

Being fully present while playing can mean that the time at recess flies by and that all-too-suddenly it is time to go back to class. This presence can also translate into a sense of connection and attunement in a game that allows you to anticipate your teammate's next move, enabling you to pass to the space they are moving to, knowing what they are going to do even before they do it. Equanimity, the mental calmness and composure that can result from playing this way, can be especially important in navigating challenging situations.

Adults also need students to "pay attention" sometimes—for example, to take in instructions. Helping students to know when and how to focus by giving them signals and the opportunity to practice shifting their attention can contribute measurably to their executive functioning. This includes skills such as adaptable thinking, planning, time management, and organization. Making the experience of learning these skills fun and creating associations for them that are positive has been demonstrated to have a significant positive impact.[19]

Small
Start:

Another playful set of rituals that help students build the muscle of focus are **Signals** or **Attention-Getters**. Signals are any sound or body movement that initiates an action for a group. Common signals are a whistle, clapping, two fingers raised in the air, call and response, or a verbal cue. Some signals are used to stop action, some to start action, and others to create breaks and transitions between activities. We have found that having a clear signal or set of signals is imperative when working with groups of children. By using attention getters and signals you can leverage your students energy and volume to help them focus themselves.

Some of our favorite signals include Superhero pose (in which everyone freezes in the stance of a Superhero), the musical "Shave and Haircut" call and response, the rhythmic clapping (that Lamar modeled previously), and **Match Me,** which strangely seems to work better the more quietly it's done, with the leader doing a series of different motions like touching her shoulders and her knees and her nose, instructing "Match Me" with each step.

Throw
Like a Girl

18

Hector Salazar, our former coach who now leads Reading Partners in the Bay Area, tells a great story of a dad who had been hesitant about his daughter participating in our girls' basketball league until the Cal Women's basketball team showed up to run a clinic. Seeing the diverse, powerful, and talented women working with his daughter and her teammates, and describing their experiences as scholar athletes at Cal, Hector said you could watch the father's whole understanding shift. After the clinic the father approached Hector and said, simply, "I want *that* for my daughter."

Power of
Play:

It's taken us some time as a culture to accept, include, and support girls and women in sports, but the shift in attitudes that I have witnessed over the past 25 years has been remarkable. And although launching a girls' basketball league at Sports4Kids was not initially the obvious thing to do, it ended up being one of the most important experiences in our history.

Sports4Kids was pretty small during our first couple of years—one coach at two different schools the first year, seven coaches the second year, and 14 coaches the third. We attracted a mix of people—men and women, ethnically and racially diverse. And although our program was immediately well received by school staff members and students, there was still one thing that really troubled us: no matter which staff person was out at recess, the boys were disproportionately likely to jump into whatever activity we were offering.

In reflecting on our gender challenge out at recess, I was reminded of a book I had read in college: Carol Gilligan's *In a Different Voice*.[20] There are some books that have an outsized impact on your life, and Gilligan's book was that for me. In my defense, Harvard University Press called it "the little book that started a revolution." When I read it in the early 1980s, just shortly after it had been published, I was an impressionable college sophomore, and it struck me as wholly different from anything I had ever read before.

In the book, Gilligan makes the argument that traditional discussions of moral development focused on a "principled way" of reasoning, as opposed to centering relationships, and that this inherently privileged the male approach. In other words, Gilligan was making the case that historic interpretations of right and wrong had been reverse engineered to focus on how guys do it.

How, you might reasonably ask, does this have anything to do with recess? When I noticed that boys were disproportionately playing in our program, I wondered if it was the result of how we structured the activities. Gilligan's theory was that boys' decisions were more defined by the activity itself and by separation, and girls were more likely to make choices and decisions grounded in relationships. It made me wonder: would the girls be more likely to join our activities if they could do so as part of a team?

Although this line of questioning feels fairly obvious in retrospect, I think it's an extremely important aspect of how we have always built programs at Playworks and another essential lesson of play. Rather than assuming that it was somehow the girls' fault that they weren't participating, we looked at how the games were set up for clues as to how we might redesign them to promote inclusion. Play lends itself well to this kind of adaptation, offering lots of useful insights in this moment as we are considering how best to reimagine education to foster belonging. Fundamentally, this is how we achieve equity.

So we decided to start a girls' basketball league. We had some help. My former JV college basketball coach, Missy Park, had started the women's athletic wear company Title 9 Sports, and she was interested in finding a way for her employees to be involved in the community. Title 9 provided funding and its staff worked alongside ours as coaches and referees.

Right from the start, the league was a huge success. The girls loved it, the families loved it, and our staff members loved it. The school staff members were blown away by the levels of engagement, and we heard from principals that they were coming to the games because there was more family involvement in our leagues than in any other school activity. School secretaries showed up to cheer their teams on and not a few custodians confessed that although initially bent out of shape that they had to stay late, they had been surprised to discover how much they enjoyed the games.

For the most part, none of the girls had ever really played basketball before. Sure, they'd seen it on television or in the neighborhood, but we were starting very much with the basics in terms of dribbling, passing, and shooting—let alone trying to do all three of these things in some sort of coherent order. Although these were low-scoring affairs, the abundance of joy, the thrill of the crowd, and the sheer delight that ensued when something went right made games surprisingly exciting. There were lots of moments when girls would just take off running with the ball, completely forgetting to dribble because they were unable to contain their excitement at having caught the pass. And each game involved someone shoot-ing into the wrong basket, often more than once.

We debated making accommodations to make it easier for the girls to reach the hoop, but the availability of adjustable baskets was too uneven, and we decided that it put too much emphasis on the score. The range of sizes among fourth- and fifth-grade girls was really quite notable when on display in this setting. There were girls who were full-sized women and girls who were tiny, but they themselves didn't really seem too worried about their differences, or even particularly aware of them. Parents or coaches might some-times grumble about things not being fair, but the girls always seemed happy just to be playing.

Play promotes Gender Equity

Twenty-five years is simultaneously a long time and just a blip, but if there is one area that feels like it has noticeably changed in the time that we've been running our programs, it would be attitudes about girls' participation in sport. When we first started running pro-grams, the expectation was that there were boys' activities—basketball, soccer, football—and girls' activities—four square, jump rope, and imaginary play. There were always girls who played in the "boys' activities" and boys who played in the "girls' activities," but there were judgments that accompanied these decisions, and the derision was generally more critical of the boys participating in activities considered female. More than once a teacher or custodian or volunteer parent tried to actively discourage a boy at one of our schools from jumping rope—an activity that seemed to really disturb them.

A first step in undoing these stereotypes may have included us having a particularly athletic male coach jump rope, but the influence of a shifting popular media has had an undeniably profound effect as well. Over the past 25 years, opportunities to watch women playing competitive sports other than gymnastics and ice-skating have exploded. Women's college and professional basketball are regularly on television, and women's soccer—at least at the internationally competitive level—has a higher viewership than men's soccer in the US.

Another significant shift that we've experienced is related to changing attitudes about homosexuality and gender identity. Because play is a space where kids are making meaning of the world around them, and a space where kids often feel freer to ask questions than they might in other situations, our staff members have been placed in a position of wrestling with how best to respond to questions such as, "Do you have a boyfriend?" or "Are you a boy or a girl?"

Jo Doyle is a former coach and trainer who tells a story of being out on the playground when a student asked the question, "Coach, are you a boy or a girl?" Jo, who had been struggling with their gender identity at the time, paused before answering. Just then a second grader interjected with, "My mom used to be my dad and she says whenever you're not sure and to be polite you can use *they/them* pronouns so we can call you a *they/them,* Coach." The second grader then ran off to play a different game, the other kids nodded in acceptance, and our coach was left standing there, reeling from the profound simplicity and mind-boggling acceptance of this group of young students. Jo has claimed *they/them* and has lived as nonbinary ever since.

Although there is still cruelty and unease with a broader interpretation of gender identity, the familiarity that play affords—the opportunities that it creates for people to truly see others and to feel truly seen—is a critical precursor to expanding acceptance and understanding.

Small
Start:

Although **Language** has a powerful influence in all aspects of life, paying special attention to how language is exclusionary about gender is especially important. Beyond encouraging our staff members to be respectful of how individuals identify and to seek guidance in the use of pronouns, we also ask that our staff members be mindful of two particular language missteps that hinder inclusion.

First: Avoid using phrases like "you guys."

BEFORE: "Ok, I want <u>you guys</u> who want to play basketball to line up on the baseline. . . ."

Now: "Ok, I want <u>everyone</u> who wants to play basketball to line up on the baseline. . . ."

Before: "<u>You guys</u> did a great job in the game today."

Now: "<u>You all</u> did a great job in the game today."

Second: Reframe the instructions so that they aren't making exceptions for girls.

Before: "In order to be fair and make sure everyone touches the ball, a girl must receive one pass in a series in order for the point to count."

Now: "To work on our teamwork and passing, five passes must be made to different players before a team can score a point."

Leveling the Playing Field 19

Throughout this book I've included various stories to exemplify the many aspects of play's influence, but I could not help but notice in looking back over all of them that race played a role. There have been other factors—discrimination based on gender, class, native language—that have affected our ability to deliver effective programming—but the issue of racism stands apart. In America, race is defining in our economic, political, and educational systems. After 25 years of running Playworks, I am convinced that it won't be possible for us to achieve our mission unless we make significant progress as a nation in addressing the legacy of racism, and more specifically in tackling the impacts of unconscious bias in schools. It is only through fundamentally reorienting our social norms to dismantle white privilege that we can begin to address all the other forms of discrimination that prevent our children from being whole.

Power of Play:

It has been my experience as a White woman leading Playworks that not only do the dynamics of race affect the experience of play, play also creates important opportunities for addressing the dynamics of race. Play has everything to teach us about redressing the racial inequities in our country because it helps us to feel comfortable moving forward imperfectly. While building trust and empathy and resilience, play is the experiential way we come to truly understand that anything worth doing is worth doing poorly—at least initially—in order to get better at it. Play is the place where kids learn, as Coach Hector once said to me, "If you do wrong, you can make it right." Talking about race, understanding how it shows up, and exploring ways of challenging these inequities requires exactly this attitude of willingness, curiosity, and experimentation. To paraphrase Dante and quote Robert Frost, "the only way out is through."

In their excellent book, *Unconscious Bias in Schools*, Tracey Benson and Sarah Fiarman make the observation that one of the biggest challenges for educators in addressing unconscious bias is the simple fact that grown-ups who are trying to help find it very hard to reconcile the idea that they may be unwittingly causing harm.[21] Grappling with this understanding, no matter how unpleasant or threatening it is to one's sense of self, is necessary if unconscious bias is to be addressed. Just as we considered how changing the nature of our program might encourage greater participation by girls, creating a more racially equitable environment requires that we stop the practice of seeing the deficit in children and begin shifting accountability for the situation to our own practices as adults.

Although data on recess-specific disciplinary actions are limited, the research on disproportionate discipline—the practice of subjecting specific demographic groups (e.g., race/ethnicity, sex, disability status) to particular disciplinary actions at a greater rate than students who belong to other demographic groups—is definitive. According to the School Discipline Support Initiative, children of color are significantly more likely than their White peers to be disciplined, boys more likely than girls, and the severity of punishment for the same infraction varies dramatically, with Black children more likely to receive a harsher response.[22] This issue of severity is connected to racially biased practices, including zero-tolerance discipline, that are more frequently applied to Black and Latinx students. Additionally, the patterns of discipline referrals reflect that although White students are more likely to be referred to the office for more objectively observed infractions such as vandalizing or making obscene comments, Black students were more likely to be referred to the office for more subjective infractions such as being disrespectful or making too much noise.[23]

Patterns of disproportionate discipline aren't exclusive to educating older students and, in fact, are actually worse in preschool, with suspension rates that are three times higher than students in kindergarten through grade 12. In 2014, the US Department of

Education released the results of its 2012 Civil Rights Data Collection, reporting that Black children, who comprise only 18 percent of the preschool population, make up nearly half of all preschool suspensions. American Indian and Native Alaskan students represent less than 1% of the student population but up to 3% of suspensions and expulsions.[24]

Not surprisingly, all of this is evident on the playground as well. Because the playground is an environment in which students have more latitude to run around and express themselves, it creates more opportunities for unconscious bias to manifest among the grown-ups tasked with managing it. Attitudes and expectations about "appropriate behaviors" that are racially based play out in ways that prompt educators to treat different students differently. Rough-housing that might be gently discouraged for a group of White students is interpreted as more dangerous when the students are Black; an acerbic comment from an Asian girl is interpreted as somehow less rude than the same words from a Black girl.

Precisely because the playground is a place where our biases are so evident, it represents a tremendous opportunity to consciously address these patterns. When schools hold themselves accountable to paying attention to the ways they treat students differently, they can begin to address these discrepancies. This is a great potential application of the insight that *what we measure matters*. When we begin to actually keep track of who loses recess and for what, who gets detention and how often, and who gets suspended and why, we begin to see patterns that can be addressed and change is made possible.

Unconscious bias on the playground also has a direct and significant impact on what happens in the classroom. Even when adults are not formally tracking patterns of discipline, you can be fairly certain that our students are paying close attention. These students are making meaning of their observations, which impacts how they see themselves and authority, and (understandably and justifiably) affects their sense of trust and resilience. Education does not happen in a vacuum, and a teacher's expectations of a student influence his or her interactions and consequently a child's experience and performance for better and for worse.

Play promotes
Racial Equity

One of the best things about working with kids, and sometimes one of the most jarring things about working with them, is their lack of well-developed filters. Kids will often say the things that adults are thinking but are conditioned not to say aloud. I mentioned previously the experience when Bob Lujano visited a school, and the students commented audibly on his absence of arms and legs— much to the horror of the grown-ups present. And I mentioned the students asking Coach Jo whether they were a boy or a girl. Kids can be similarly direct about race. Although sometimes this is done out of actual lack of knowledge, sometimes there can be an element of cruelty involved, mimicking something they may have picked up from an adult in their life or from popular culture.

When a comment along these lines happens, it is telling to watch how grown-ups respond. Over the years we've noticed that the response tends to be one of two types—either the grown-up in earshot pretends not to have heard the comment or the grown-up goes completely ballistic. Unfortunately, both of these responses preclude maximizing these moments as opportunities to help students deepen their understanding of what they have said, what it means, and how it affects others.

Moments like these deserve serious attention, and how we as grown-ups respond sends important messages to the students who are the actors as well as those at whom the action or comment has been directed. Pretending not to hear comments, although an understandable response because of either fatigue or fear of getting it wrong, is a form of inaction that speaks as loudly as any action might. And reacting dramatically, again, totally understandable because of the strong feelings racism elicits, nonetheless shuts down conversations that could potentially lead to greater understanding. Extreme reactions, especially in response to comments made by younger students, can end up being profoundly confusing. Students learn from the world around them and make sense of what they hear by repeating information in order to learn more. This does not mean that they don't need to take responsibility for the impact their words have, but only in acknowledging the presence of systemic racism and by being willing to name it and talk about it do we have an opportunity to undo it.

Doing this in a skillful way is not easy. The playground offers an opportunity, however, to proactively develop these skills. By inviting students to play in games that break down the patterns of segregation on a schoolyard that tend to form—for example, inviting Latinx kids to play basketball—we can call out these stereotypes and challenge them. Giving students a chance to voice and question these assumptions in an environment that isn't charged, with an adult who is prepared and willing to support the conversation, can lead to greater understanding.

Having laid a foundation like this, our staff members have found that it then becomes easier to engage when more challenging situations arise, such as overtly racist name-calling or insults. In asking why someone would make a comment about another person's race and if they understand why it is hurtful, it has been our experience that often students will acknowledge that they have said things without fully understanding the meaning of their words, repeating something they have heard an adult say, from music lyrics, or that they picked up online. More serious infractions require engaging the administration and communicating with families, but first and foremost our goal as educators should be promoting understanding.

Mitigating unconscious bias through play may seem like a stretch, but play is our one universal experience in which we actually have practice—and success—creating *level playing fields*. Whether it is through changing the rules while in the middle of a game or in the act of shifting team members, play is an exercise in designing for equity. It is hard to point to other domains where we so expressly value the closest, most competitive contests and where, on any given day, any team might win because there is an equal distribution of talent and resources. Play may be the one domain where we genuinely believe that a level playing field is *the essential precondition* for real greatness to shine through—sometimes from our stars, but more often through the collective effort of the team as a whole.

Staffing

Over the years one of the most common requests that we have gotten from principals when assigning staff members to a school is that we send a man of color. Although Playworks has had a high number of male staff members of color relative to many other educational organizations, we are not exclusively staffed thusly and so the request has also been an important prompt for a broader discussion about what students need.

The request does make sense. The data are categorical that having one teacher of the same race has a significant impact on student achievement, and having two makes an even bigger difference. Researchers in Tennessee found that Black students matched with a Black kindergarten teacher were as much as 18 percent more likely than their peers to enroll in college. And a 2017 study found that having just one Black teacher in elementary school decreased the risk of Black boys from low-income backgrounds dropping out of high school by nearly 40 percent.[25]

But when majority White organizations seek to hire Black men to act as disciplinarians and uncompensated mentors, it sets up a racially inequitable environment for Black staff members. It is worth considering how acknowledging this dynamic raises important questions about how we design staff roles and how we compensate in light of the unspoken responsibilities and expectations put on Black staff members or other staff members of color.

For optimal education experiences, students need role models in whom they see themselves *and* positive diversity experiences— constructive interactions and discussions, meaningful friendships, and positive shared experiences across different races, ethnicities, religions, and genders. The absence of negative diversity experiences—in other words, not having one's ideas or opinions shut down because of one's racial, religious, or gender identity, or hurtful, unresolved interactions with diverse students or staff—is also closely associated with a broad range of positive outcomes.

Play's ability to help us build the skills needed to manage social connection is foundational to navigating the dynamics of race and more specifically to mitigating potentially negative experiences. Truly creating an environment in which all students have choice and voice is critical to redressing unconscious bias. By increasing students' problem-solving skills, you can avoid minor conflicts ("the ball was in"—"you were tagged") from crowding out the time and energy required for addressing more significant issues that will arise on the playground. Play fosters an environment that centers belonging, which is essential to schools being places where dynamics of racism are not allowed to go unaddressed.

We ask Playworks' staff members to be the grown-ups out on the yard who don't turn away when they overhear a comment that is racist, sexist, anti-Semitic, homophobic, or otherwise unkind. This requires a significant level of self-awareness and the necessary energy to hold challenging conversations. Being the adult who addresses these questions is a big responsibility, and we try our best to ensure that our staff members have the resources and support they need to do this well, while also taking care of themselves. We recognize that for staff members who are people of color, this responsibility can be overwhelming, even when it is happening in the seemingly less-charged environment of play. The persistent demands of attending to the feelings and interpretations of White coworkers, concerns about being perceived as somehow angry or unreasonable, and the gas-lighting experience of living in a world where systemic racism feels blindingly obvious and consistently denied create an additional burden. It is incumbent on White staff to recognize the unfair burden that addressing racial inequity places on colleagues of color and to step up when issues arise.

Small
Start:

We've talked about transitions and facilitation throughout this book, but there is one specific aspect of these two practices that merits a special call-out, especially as a tool in supporting equity work: **Reflection**. As a general rule, we are kind of lame as a species in terms of giving feedback and debriefing, which is deeply problematic given that it makes such a huge difference in how we makes sense of things. If you've ever watched a really great coach or teacher, the one thing that they often do better than their peers is prompt reflection by their players or students that enable them to really understand—to see for themselves—the connections and meaning in their learning.

Leading students in Reflection activities related to play is a critical step in ensuring that play's benefits are able to take root. Inviting feedback on what went well and what was challenging during a game or activity prompts the kind of engagement that is associated with belonging. And Reflection doesn't have to just happen at the end of an experience. When introducing a new game, consider integrating mid-game questions so players can reflect on what they practiced or when they might play the game next. Try these or use your own: What was challenging about the game? What did you need to do to be successful? What do you think this game teaches? When would be a good time to play this game? How does this promote teamwork? How does this promote inclusion? What might you try next time?

Getting Better 20

Social-emotional learning (SEL) and family wellness have been embedded in the curriculum of the Washoe County School District in Nevada for nearly a decade, and they have been a partner with Playworks integrating play into this approach. When the northern Nevada school system closed its 107 schools in mid-March 2020 because of the coronavirus pandemic and shifted to distance learning, the continuation of SEL lessons became a priority. Feedback from schools and families suggest that the daily SEL lessons built strong relationships and encouraged talk about emotional wellness. Importantly, as the district looked to reopen, SEL and play, along with other wrap-around services that contribute to good mental health and wellness, were considered an essential aspect of the school day for not only students but staff as well. "The number one priority, beyond the physical safety, beyond the social distancing, beyond the PPE [personal protective equipment] needs," Superintendent Kristen McNeill says, "is going to have to be about the mental health of our students and the mental health of our staff."

Power of
Play:

Play helps us connect. By creating a sense of familiarity, play leads to greater trust and rapport that can help lower the automatic responses of the ego and other misplaced survival instincts that can be problematic in establishing healthy connection. Just as play helps young people become more comfortable with the truth of our interdependence, playful activities for adults can contribute to a greater awareness and acceptance of how much we need one another to actually thrive.

As schools have been reopening, we have been doing our best to support them in exploring how play might be a critical piece of the puzzle. Although there is a general recognition that students' social and emotional needs require a re-entry process that is designed to support a more gradual re-introduction of routines and an empha- sis on building trust and connection, the actual logistics of how this will be achieved are still fuzzy. Balancing this need with the pressure to achieve academic remediation is challenging, and adding com- plication to this dynamic is a general uncertainty about how social distancing and hybrid learning will affect the process. Reimagining the spaces for play—and for learning more broadly—will be a critical step in designing a workable environment for teaching and learning.

The human impulse is to look at a situation and to jump immediately to problem-solving, skipping the important step of adequately assessing the situation. We are fixers by nature, and solving the wrong problem, or solving the problem that we feel most comfortable with, or the problem we know how to solve, are all too common human behaviors that often as not can make a situation worse. Rather than rushing to solve the myriad problems that lie before us, this moment calls for an investment in our resilience.

Play contributes to our sense of resilience by helping young people learn to navigate human connection and, just as importantly, disconnection. The pandemic has highlighted the underlying weaknesses of our social support systems as social isolation and depression among young people have reached epidemic proportions. Returning to school will require creating environments that can support students and educators as they navigate this transition, while also addressing the traumas that many will have sustained. The beautiful trappings of play—the rituals, rules, and referees—will be essential to create the order and predictability that will make reconnecting possible. Just as play is a tool for children to initially develop the skills that enable them to manage social connections, it represents a powerful—and much-needed—opportunity for them to rebuild these muscles.

Play helps us
Heal

Trauma-informed practices reinforce this understanding. On a site visit to see the Playworks in action, Nadine Burke Harris, California's surgeon general, noted that the program seemed "almost designed" to support students who had experienced trauma. There are three main conditions that we focus on that enable all students to thrive: we give students choice and voice, we place a focused attention on transitions, and we provide a caring and consistent grown-up who has the bandwidth to resist reacting negatively when a student acts out.

There is much that we need in this moment: the ability to work across difference, the humility to recognize where we have been wrong, the strength to forgive, the curiosity to learn, the faith that things will get better if we try, and the collective will to make the changes that we so desperately need.

My friend Marc Freedman turned me on to a wonderful quote from his former mentor John Gardner, "What we have before us are some breathtaking opportunities disguised as insoluble problems."

Although Gardner said this in 1965, his words feel just as true today, reminding us that America has always been an aspiration as much as anything. In this moment as we are figuring out how to come back from the devastating personal and economic implications of the COVID-19 pandemic, while also wrestling with the profound inequities that these crises have laid bare, I choose to hear his words as an invitation to embrace the moment as an impetus to actually be better than we were before.

Small
Start:

One of my all-time favorite games to lead in large crowds as the ultimate closer is called **RoShamBo Rockstar**. Essentially, it's a giant, single-elimination Rock-Paper-Scissors tournament, in which an ever-diminishing number of victors are supported by an ever-growing crowd of their recently vanquished opponents. Ultimately the game is reduced to two final remaining contestants with roughly half the group behind each of them now cheering wildly.

The biggest group I ever led in this activity was a 1,600-person America's Promise conference held in a massive Washington, DC, convention center. At the end of my talk, I asked everyone to rise and to identify a partner. I explained the rules to RoShamBo Rockstar and that we were going to play, here and now, in the convention center. There was a stunned silence. But I persisted, explaining that because of the magic of math, it would go more quickly than they were imagining, and that if it made them more comfortable, they could think of it as a giant performance art piece deconstructing the fleeting nature of leadership. To my great relief, they stood and started playing. And it worked! They laughed and moved around, somewhat awkwardly navigating the tables in the cavernous space, but cheering wildly and winning and losing until, about six minutes later, it came down to the two final contestants: a high school student and the former mayor of Philadelphia, Wilson Goode. The two finalists were brought up to the stage and, much to the delight of the crowd, after three rounds of both contestants throwing out rock, the young woman defeated the elder statesman.

Notes

1   Fisher, Daniel, and Julia Freeland Fisher. *Who You Know: Unlocking Innovations That Expand Students' Networks*. Jossey-Bass, 2018.

2   You can watch his speech at: https://www.laureus.com/news/celebrating-the-legacy-of-a-hero-on-mandela-day.

3   Sorry, I had to throw in just a little more play theory: Groos, Karl. *The Play of Animals*. Chapman and Hall, 1898.

4   Check out the videos of these claps at www.playworks.org/whyplayworksgameguide.

5   Goleman, Daniel. *Emotional Intelligence*. Bantam Books, 1995.

6   Goleman, Daniel. *Primal Leadership*. Harvard Business Review Press, 2004.

7   Schmitz, Paul. *Everyone Leads: Building Leadership from the Community Up*. Jossey-Bass, 2011.

8   powell, john a. "Editor's Introduction." *Othering and Belonging Journal* 1.

9   Massey, W. V., M. B. Stellino, S. P. Mullen, et al. "Development of the Great Recess Framework—Observational Tool to Measure Contextual and Behavioral Components of Elementary School Recess." *BMC Public Health* 18, 394 (2018). https://doi.org/10.1186/s12889-018-5295-y.

10   Strauss, Valerie. "Being Safe and Feeling Safe Aren't The Same Thing—and the Difference Will Matter to Kids When Schools Open." *Washington Post* (July 8, 2020). https://www.washingtonpost.com/education/2020/07/08/

being-safe-feeling-safe-arent-same-thing-difference-will-matter-kids-when-schools-open/.

11   K12Lab.org/safety.

12   Skenazy, Lenore. "Why I Let My 9-Year-Old Ride the Subway Alone." *New York Sun,* 2008.

13   Ekelund, Ulf, et al. "Physical Activity and All-Cause Mortality across Levels of Overall and Abdominal Adiposity in European Men and Women: The European Prospective Investigation into Cancer and Nutrition Study (EPIC)." *The American Journal of Clinical Nutrition* 101, 3 (March 2015): 613–621. https://doi.org/10.3945/ajcn.114.100065.

14   Ratey, John. *Spark: The Revolutionary New Science of Exercise and the Brain.* Little, Brown, 2008.

15.   CDC, "Physical Education." https://www.cdc.gov/healthyschools/physicalactivity/physical-education.htm.

16   Sanchez-Vaznaugh, E. V., M. O'Sullivan, and S. Egerter. "When School Districts Fail to Comply with State Physical Education Laws, the Fitness of California's Children Lags." A Policy Brief. Active Living Research, December 2013.

17   Bridges, William. *Transitions.* DaCapo Lifelong Books, 1979.

18   Csikszentmihalyi, Mihaly. *Flow: The Psychology of Optimal Experience.* HarperPerennial, 1991.

19   Singer, Dorothy G., Roberta Michnick Golinkoff, and Kathy Hirsh-Pasek, eds. *Play=Learning: How Play Motivates and Enhances Children's Cognitive and Social-Emotional Growth.* Oxford University Press, 2006.

20   Gilligan, Carol. *In a Different Voice.* Harvard University Press, 1982.

21   Benson, Tracey, and Sarah Fiarman. *Unconscious Bias in Schools: A Developmental Approach to Exploring Race and Racism.* Harvard Education Press, 2020.

22   https://supportiveschooldiscipline.org/.

23   https://www.air.org/project/conditions-learning-survey.

24   US Department of Education Office for Civil Rights. "CIVIL RIGHTS DATA COLLECTION Data Snapshot." School Discipline Issue Brief No. 1 (March 2014).

25   "Black Teachers Improve Outcomes for Black Students." *U.S. News & World Report,* November 2018.

We Can
Do This

Although I started Playworks to ensure daily play in children's lives, I stayed at Playworks for almost 25 years because of its impact on grown-ups. Looking back at all the ground we have covered in this book—all the foundational big ideas behind play as well as all the big changes that the small starts with play can catalyze—I am convinced that there is a powerful and important role for adults in promoting play. Not surprisingly, I am also convinced that although this advocacy of play is important for kids, we lucky grown-ups who take it on will benefit just as much, if not more, as the kids for whom we are advocating.

We've looked at why you should care about play, and we've talked a lot about what you can achieve through play. This final section of the book is my parting gift: some thoughts on how you might go about making it happen. This is a pick-your-own adventure situation, and to ensure that everyone can find an approach that works for them, I offer suggestions and insights in four flavors: play yourself, infuse play, protect play, and advocate play.

Before we jump in, though, I want to offer two critical insights about being an effective champion for play. First, whenever possible, let kids lead. It may not work to start with kids out in front—you may need to set the stage and help them learn the rules and develop the skills they need to navigate the situation successfully—but having the ultimate goal that students will be the leaders and drivers of their own play as your north star goes a long way toward setting you up for success.

The second insight is don't lose your sense of humor. You can take the work seriously, but to the extent humanly possible, it helps if you try not to take *yourself* too seriously. There will be ups and downs, and sometimes it may feel as though "no good deed goes unpunished," but this is all going to go a lot better if you remember to laugh and roll with whatever comes and, above all else, be kind.

Play Yourself

In 2015–2016, I spent a year as a fellow at Stanford's Hasso Plattner Institute of Design, known more colloquially as the d.school. It was an extraordinary opportunity to learn about human-centered design—to be fully immersed in it—by digging into an idea, a question actually. My question was, "How might we redesign the substitute teaching experience?" As the fellowship started, I was excited to jump into the new material, and I imagined that in this return to school, I would be reading about theory in conjunction with heady discussions about my area of inquiry—and those of my fellow fellows. To the contrary, we spent the first two weeks of the fellowship essentially playing together.

One of the earliest experiences was participating in the d.school's popular Executive Education Design Thinking Bootcamp. This is one of those corporate education programs that for-profit companies pay for all the time, and the fellows and I got to come along for the ride. The bootcamp kicked off with an introduction to "stokes" (warm-up activities designed to boost energy, build connection, foster empathy, support collaboration, and cultivate creativity), many of which were actually games that Playworks staff play with elementary school students. I was only a little surprised when the high-level executives jumped right in. As a participant, I played alongside and was fascinated to watch as these new colleagues laughed and High-Fived, as they cringed at their own completely inconsequential "mistakes," and then quickly returned to playing. Working with the bootcamp participants for that short period, and building deeper relationships with the d.school fellows over that year, was greatly facilitated by the connections we built through play.

My d.school experience taught me a lot, but in many ways what it really did was help me make meaning of past lessons. The d.school helped me to clarify and articulate what I had learned from years of watching adults wake up to the power of play simply by playing with children and each other. In part, this was possible because of the tools and mindsets the d.school uses, but it was also possible because my fellowship year allowed for undirected time and space to make sense of the things I was learning. In other words, not only was the direct use of play in building relationships a critical part of the process, the more nuanced experience of play as any activity undertaken for no apparent purpose also contributed directly.

George Bernard Shaw is thought to have said, "We don't stop playing because we grow old; we grow old because we stop playing."

From risk-taking to social norming, grown-ups at play exhibit the same range of delights and frustrations as their younger selves. Although actions such as self-handicapping and conflict resolution may be more challenging the older we get, the context of play can be an opportunity that stands outside of regular life and serves as a reminder of all that is possible. Now, after so many years of encouraging adults to play alongside kids, I am convinced that play is a critical, and often overlooked, tool for promoting the kind of trust and connection that is so desperately needed in all of our lives, especially in this moment in our culture.

Silly as a Superpower

One of the interesting contradictions of adults and play is that in enabling people to take themselves less seriously, you make it possible for them to take their work and those around them more seriously. Being silly is a great way to get there.

In many of the interviews I did with former Playworks staff, the importance of silliness came up. Amy Jones, a former coach who is now the principal at a Playworks school, talked about being silly as a strategy for breaking through to people, getting their attention, and easing their worries. Although she was clear that play and silly were not a complete overlap—Amy might well be one of the most competitive people I know, and playing basketball with her is not a silly experience—they are inextricably intertwined. In Amy's telling, silly is a super power. As a principal struggling to maintain engagement during the pandemic, Amy relied on weekly all-school meetings where she would sing, wear costumes, and basically do whatever it took to create the hook to inspire the most disconnected in her community to keep calling in.

Silly is also a well-documented strategy for sparking and accessing creativity. One of the brainstorming techniques that the d.school encourages is to begin an idea generation process by spending five minutes thinking of ways to solve a given problem with solutions that involve magic, cost a million dollars or more, are illegal, or involve David Hasselhoff. These obviously outrageous parameters invite participants to more effectively let go of pre-existing biases, to internalize the idea that no suggestion is out of bounds, and to shake us out of our usual distracted state, encouraging a level of engagement and connection with others that, more often than not, makes the whole greater than the sum of its parts.

* * *

Which brings us back to Johan Huizinga and his book *Homo Ludens*. Admittedly, Huizinga isn't everyone's cup of tea. He's best known for having written *The Waning of the Middle Ages*, the classic 1919 study of the medieval period in France and the Netherlands.[1] Some people were surprised that he turned his attention to play with *Homo Ludens,* although his treatment of chivalry and its implications for medieval life were likely inspiration for his insights. According to Huizinga, the central function of play in a flourishing society is in providing structure and rules that inspire participants who are willing to be creative within the pre-scribed boundaries. Huizinga's take on play is *very* adult.

One of my favorite passages in Huizinga's book is when he com-pares our engagement in the play state with the sacred. He likens the suspension of the regular rules that play requires with the taking of the sacrament, describing in spiritual terms the change in awareness and connection with others that happens when we step into the boundaries of a game. He's not alone in connecting play to the spiritual. The Dalai Lama has also called out play as a critical human trait, essential to our emotional, physical, and spiritual well-being. He himself will not infrequently do silly things while giving talks and lectures, giggling infectiously and celebrating the power of play to promote empathy, kindness, and perspective.

Although Huizinga and the Dalai Lama demonstrate a deep reverence for playfulness, their perspectives stand apart from the more commonly held attitude toward play, particularly in the United States. Our ambivalence about playfulness is especially evident when judging adult behavior. Although we are drawn to people who are exuberant, playfulness is still equated with being childlike at best, and, more critically, as a reflection of immaturity.

This is a huge lost opportunity. At Playworks, our experiences in playfully training and supporting adults has demonstrated that this propensity to dismiss play in grown-ups is harmful. Playful professionalism is not only a more enjoyable way to navigate work but also a powerful tool for promoting a healthy workplace culture, one that is marked by the presence of trust and a comfort with, and an openness to, learning from mistakes. These qualities are indispensable to creativity and innovation. Contrary to the perception of play as a sign of immaturity, playfulness can reflect a mature mindset that enables us to interact effectively with others.

Our ambivalence about play sometimes results in a reticence to participate in playful activities. Professionals worry they will look foolish. In the case of educators, hesitancy in participation sometimes comes out of concern that they may somehow lose control of the situation if they let down their guard. At other times it is the direct result of actual prohibitions against adults taking part. In any case, the key to making play more comfortable for adults—just as it is with students—is in centering choice and voice. As we have discussed, it isn't play if it's not voluntary, and this holds true no matter how old someone is.

Playing yourself—whether you are a teacher, a parent, a coach, or just a member of the community—has an impact on the world beyond you. Valuing and modeling play changes its worth in the eyes of the children in your life, but societally as well. Prioritizing play with your time and energy and attention sends an important message to those around you about your values and influences community perception of the importance of play for others.

American culture places an inflated value on *apparent* purpose. We have an almost obsessive relationship with being "busy" (or at least appearing to be so) and to *doing* something as opposed to simply *being*. Although some degree of busyness is associated with positive outcomes—a greater sense of self-importance, which can increase self-control—too much busyness is connected to negative impacts as well. The compunction to be excessively busy is associated with chronic stress and skyrocketing rates of anxiety and depression in young people. Engaging in play is a proactive way to fend off the false glamour of busy and to make a strong statement about the things you really value. Modeling this for the kids around you sets them up to create lives where they spend their time in ways that reflect what they really care about.

Infuse Play

If you take away nothing else from this book, I hope it is the idea that play can and should be infused into any activity. There is always a way to respectfully bring a little play to bear in any situation as an invitation to people to be a little more present, a little more authentic, a little more connected, and a little more engaged. As someone who works or spends time with kids—be that as a teacher, parent, coach, counselor, or after-school provider—creatively infusing play into whatever you are doing not only makes life much easier but also sets up the children you care about for success, short term and for life.

A few years ago, Playworks had a partnership with the National Head Start Association that gave us an opportunity to run some joint trainings for families and Head Start teachers. Working with the families was particularly gratifying because we were able to introduce lots of games that helped make basic parenting tasks easier. Turning clean up into a mini basketball game or playing follow the leader to help with an otherwise challenging transition at the beginning of the day provided joyful tweaks to family routines. We heard repeatedly from the participating families that the workshops were a relief because they reminded them of all the ways they already intuitively knew how to be with their kids, and it gave them permission to have fun while parenting.

Even as grown-ups—maybe even especially as grown-ups—it's so easy to feel like we're doing something wrong. And in this moment when everything feels turned upside down and the risks and challenges of our day-to-day experience feel even more extreme than usual, incorporating play into daily routines helps to collectively inoculate us against the unexpected. Play helps us roll with the punches, and infusing it into activities that you are doing with kids—or other grown-ups for that matter—can contribute to a greater ease with change.

The role of a coach provides a good model for thinking about how to be an adult who champions play by intentionally infusing it into a child's experience. Being a coach, above all else, is an opportunity to build a caring culture—or, as Jim Thompson, founder of Positive Coaching Alliance (PCA), puts it, "the creation of a caring climate."[2] This caring climate is marked by mutual trust, respect, and connection, all enhanced through play.

Applying a coach's approach to parenting or teaching—thinking about how desired skills might be playfully broken down, combining didactic instruction with experiential learning, and interspersing opportunities for kids to joyfully experience their own progress toward mastery—raises interesting possibilities for creatively reimagining how play can be infused into other activities. Just as sports and play aren't exactly the same thing, coaching isn't an automatically playful activity. But coaching has the head start of being based in games. The experience of a coach—someone who is navigating the dynamics of competition, inclusion, and trust while working with a group of players across a spectrum of ability and skill (not unlike teachers)—is well served by focusing on play's central lesson: *it matters how it feels*.

Protect Play

A key role for adults in promoting play lies in protecting it from the many obstacles that can arise. Access limited by space, time, equity, technology, competition, gender, and adults themselves all potentially contribute as barriers to making safe and healthy play available daily. Proactively addressing these issues locally (preferably in playful and positive ways) can be critical to ensuring that every child gets to play every day.

One of the single most important things we can do to protect play is to end the practice of withholding recess. The impact of this practice is largely underreported and misunderstood. Dr. Rebecca

London, the UCSC professor introduced previously, has written extensively about this issue, referencing a survey of elementary school principals conducted by Gallup and Robert Wood Johnson Foundation in which 79 percent reported that recess was taken away as a punishment and a little more than half (54 percent) reporting that it was used as a reward.[3] London notes that although there is no research looking specifically at the impact of withholding recess, the more general research on discipline in schools applies: "punishment that excludes students can have unexpected detrimental effects, such as worsening behavior even further." London concludes, "When educators withhold a recess from children as punishment, they lose an opportunity to help students better understand the expectations of the school and to help students practice the social and emotional skills they need to be successful at recess."[4]

One of the questions that I am frequently asked in interviews is "Isn't it hard to convince 'high-performing schools' to make time for play?" The thinking, I presume, is that rigorously academic schools, independent schools, and schools where families are putting the most pressure on administrators to set their students up to get into the most competitive colleges probably don't want their kids "wasting" their time on something as frivolous as play. But the opposite is true. Kids at these 'higher performing' schools are disproportionately *more* likely to have regular access to play and sports, and it should tell us something that these schools prioritize play.

Renata Simril, CEO of LA84 (the philanthropic organization formed as the legacy of the 1984 Los Angeles Olympics), has been at the forefront of bringing awareness to play equity as reflected in inequitable access to parks, youth sports, physical activity, education, and, for the youngest children, even basic access to daily play. The work of LA84 is a model for communities everywhere. They have launched a play equity movement to extend this understanding of access to play as a social justice priority beyond their reach in the Los Angeles area.

There is a commonly held misperception that kids have equal access to play in America. That simply isn't the case. And for all the reasons we have discussed up to this point—the ways in which play contributes to health and well-being, the ways in which it helps us to assess and mitigate risk, the ways in which it helps us develop as leaders and engaged participants—not having access to play exacerbates the realities of an already inequitable society, making it that much harder for those without privilege to navigate a system that was never designed to serve them.

Advocate Play

Play advocacy has gotten increasing attention in recent years. In 2012, the United Nations issued the Convention on the Rights of Children, intended to be a benchmark against which a nation's treatment of its children might be measured. Article 31, which has come to be known as the Right to Play, reads as follows:

> That every child has the right to rest and leisure, to engage in play and recreational activities appropriate to the age of the child and to participate freely in cultural life and the arts.[5]

Although the United States signed the convention, it is the only UN member state that is not yet a party to it because this requires

Senate approval and that has not yet been sought. (You can imagine how much this upsets me.) A number of different groups—including the International Play Association—continue to advocate for US adoption, and there is hope that the Biden administration may bring the convention to the Senate for approval.

Although groups such as the Alliance for Childhood have developed strong national advocacy campaigns for access to free play in the US, the most visible advocacy efforts have been local, often focused on increasing recess minutes. One such group that formed in the mid-2010s came to be known as Florida's Recess Moms. I first met the Recess Moms when Kristi Burns, one of their members, reached out to ask for supporting research on the power of play. When Kristi moved from Northern California to Lake County, Florida, just north of Orlando, her son went from daily recess in kindergarten and first grade to no recess at all in second grade. Initially, Kristi assumed that this was just a strange oversight. She thought that if she brought the lack of recess to the attention of the right people, common sense would prevail. Such was not the case. At roughly the same time, four other moms were having similar experiences in other parts of Florida. Angela Browning, Amy Narvaez, Heather Mellet, and Roberta Brandenberg were all concerned about the lack of recess at their children's schools. These moms began to organize, coordinating visits to Tallahassee and ultimately convincing one of their state representatives to sponsor legislation. As a result of their efforts, in 2017 state legislators passed a law that requires elementary schools to set aside 20 minutes each day for "free-play recess." The group now helps organizers in other states to create their own campaigns.[6]

Beyond Florida, Missouri, New Jersey, Arizona, and Rhode Island have all passed recess laws. Seven other states—Iowa, North

Carolina, South Carolina, Louisiana, Texas, Connecticut, and Virginia—have passed requirements around daily physical activity.[7]

The American Academy of Pediatrics (AAP) has also played a significant role in advocating for play in the US. Its first report in 2007, "The Importance of Play in Promoting Healthy Child Development and Maintaining Strong Parent-Child Bonds," addressed the benefits of play as well as the trend of decreased access to play time for some children. The AAP updated this report in 2018 highlighting newer research and providing additional evidence on the critical importance of play in facilitating parent engagement; promoting safe, stable, and nurturing relationships; encouraging the development of numerous competencies, including executive functioning skills; and improving life-course trajectories.[8]

Despite these efforts, access to play remains uneven, and advocating for play in schools can be a complicated undertaking. Play never happens in a vacuum (even if it does have the magical quality that enables us to lose track of time and the world around us), and the very real constraints of schools have a defining impact on the experience. In a world in which opportunities for physical play outside of school are increasingly limited, understanding the context of education, public education in particular, and its impact on play, is critical to effectively advocating for more play in children's lives. This understanding allows for not only a strong defense of play but also a powerful offense: organized play is not only important for its own sake; it is a powerful tool in supporting educators in achieving the outcomes to which they are held accountable. Advocating for play in schools is well served by positioning it as something that not only supports our students but also helps our educators.

Working in schools is a giant lesson in the importance of context, but there are some trends that feel ubiquitous. For much of the past three decades, school culture in public education has been driven by an almost singular focus on accountability. There is much debate as to the cause of this, but most likely it was a combination of our schools being designed in response to the needs of industrialization and a frustration with persistent inequities leading to a growing focus on data-driven measures. Public education has historically exemplified the idea of a pendulum, swinging dramatically back and forth between "rigor" and "student-centered," a false choice if ever there was one. Some have suggested that prior to the outbreak of COVID-19, the pendulum was beginning to swing away from the emphasis on accountability toward a growing emphasis on the importance of social emotional learning (SEL). In any event, the advent of COVID-19 has created a very new set of circumstances that are likely to intensify the tension between a focus on emotional well-being and academic remediation.

There is an alternative approach to this moment—not either/or—but one that calls for recognition that emotional well-being leads to academic *and* social development, both of which matter now more than ever. Play is critical to this approach. Although we have much work to do—big changes are desperately needed if we are to fulfill the aspiration that is our American democracy. The most important step to take is the first one.

Start small, but start. Start playfully. You have the power, the knowledge, and the ability to make play a daily part of children's lives. I promise you that the difference this will make for these kids—in the moment and for many years to come—will astound you. And when you're feeling uncertain about how best to proceed, remember that *it matters how it feels.*

Notes

1   Huizinga, Johan. *The Waning of the Middle Ages*. Martino Publishing, 2016.

2   Fry, Mary, Chris Reid-Pinson, Susumu Iwasaki, and Jim Thompson. "Bridging Theory, Research, and Practice in Youth Sports: Sport Psychology's Partnership with Positive Coaching Alliance to Enhance Youth Sport." *Journal of Sport Psychology in Action* 11, 1 (2020): 6–19. https://doi.org/10.1080/21520704.2019.1649336.

3   "The State of Play: Gallup Survey of Principals on School Recess." Robert Wood Johnson Foundation, 2010.

4   London, Rebecca. *Rethinking Recess: Creating Safe and Inclusive Playtime for All Children in School*. Harvard Education Press, 2019.

5   International Play Association. "UN Convention on the Rights of the Child." https://ipaworld.org/childs-right-to-play/uncrc-article-31/un-convention-on-the-rights-of-the-child-1/#:~:text=%E2%80%9CThat%20every%20child%20has%20the,cultural%20life%20and%20the%20arts.

6   Clark, Kristen. "'We Started This Because of Our Kids,' Florida 'Recess Moms' Say." *Tampa Bay Times* (February 12, 2017).

7   Shammas, Brittany. "Time to Play: More State Laws Require Recess." *Edutopia* (March 7, 2019).

8   Ginsburg, Kenneth R., and the Committee on Psychosocial Aspects of Child and Family Health. "The Importance of Play in Promoting Healthy Child Development and Maintaining Strong Parent-Child Bonds." *Pediatrics* 119, 1 (January 2007): 182–191. https://doi.org/10.1542/peds.2006–2697.

Game Guide

Animal Farm

→ *Supports Self-Management, Social Awareness/Empathy*

 GROUP SIZE
6+ players

 AGE GROUP
K–3rd

 EQUIPMENT
Cones or chalk for boundaries, if needed

 TIME
5 minutes

Set Up

Designate a play area with safe boundaries and room for the group to move. An area about 20 × 20 feet should be big enough.

Before You Start

- In a circle, have children count off from 1 up to 3, 4, or 5 (depending on the size of group and complexity the group can handle).
- Assign an animal for each number, and tell players what animal they are: all 1s are dogs, 2s are ducks, and so on.
- Review with the players what sound each animal makes. They could be a dog (bark), a duck (quack), a cow (moo), a cat (meow), a sheep (baa), a lion (roar), or any other animal that makes a sound.
- Make sure each player remembers his or her animal and knows its sound.
- Review safety measures: while their eyes are closed, children walk slowly with hands out in front of them.
- Optional: assign one player to be the leader.

How to Play

- The leader starts the game. by calling out "Animal Farm, go!" or another start phrase.
- Players shut their eyes and keep them shut.
- Players make their animal sounds, and walk slowly around the area, with their hands up to act as a bumper to find their fellow matching animals.
- Once two "animals" are together, they stop moving and stay together. They continue to make their animal sounds, until the rest of their group finds them.
- The game is over when all players have found their group, or when the first group is complete and together.

Variation(s)

- Instead of numbers, give players pictures of different animals.
- Depending on the age and ability of your group, you can add more or fewer animals to make groups larger or smaller.
- After playing, have students find their animal groups later for group work during class.

Band Aid Tag

→ *Supports Social Awareness/Empathy, Decision-Making,*
Problem-Solving

 **GROUP SIZE**
10–50 players

 AGE GROUP
K–5th

EQUIPMENT
Cones or chalk for boundaries

TIME
5 minutes

Set Up

- Designate a clear playing area.
- Designate a hospital outside the play area.

Before You Start

- Demonstrate safe and gentle tagging (butterfly tags) and appropriate tagging areas (arms, back, and shoulders).
- Review what to do when tagged.
- Make sure players know where the hospital is and how to be healed—they have to do 10 jumping jacks.

How to Play

- Everyone is It.
- If players are tagged, they must take one hand and put it either directly on the spot where they were tagged or across their body on their opposite shoulder. That hand is a band aid.

- They can continue to run around trying to tag others and avoid being tagged, but they must keep their band aid on. Now they only have one free hand for tagging.
- If they are tagged again, they must take the other hand and place it on the second spot where they were tagged. They can still run around avoiding tags with both band aids on but cannot tag others.
- If they are tagged a third time, they have to go to the hospital and do 10 jumping jacks to get back in the game. These players are now healed and can again use both hands for tagging.

Variation(s)

- Players can be treated at the hospital by counting to 20 or any number up to 500, counting by 1s, 5s, 10s, or using any counting method that is age appropriate.
- Players can go to the hospital at any time to remove any band aids. They do not have to wait until they are tagged the second or third time.
- Vary the activities in the hospital for healing: crunches, 10 seconds of a dance move, saying a self-affirmation, or telling someone something that is great about yourself.

Blob Tag

→ *Supports Positive Relationships, Decision-Making, Teamwork*

 GROUP SIZE
10+ players

 AGE GROUP
1st–6th

 EQUIPMENT
Cones or chalk for boundaries

 TIME
10–15 minutes

Set Up

- Establish game boundaries.

Before You Start

- Ask for two volunteers. Assign both of them to be It. They become The Blob and must link elbows.
- Demonstrate safe tagging (gentle tags) and appropriate tagging areas (arms, back, and shoulders).
- Explain the rules, boundaries, and the importance of safety and check for understanding.
- Spread out players within playing area.

How to Play

- When play begins, The Blob moves together, keeping elbows linked, and tries to tag the rest of the players.
- When players are tagged, they link elbows with the tagger, becoming part of The Blob.
- When a fourth player is tagged, The Blob can then separate into two separate blobs.

- Every time The Blob becomes four players it can split. Two players detach creating separate blobs.
- Play continues until all of the players become part of blobs.
- If players run out of bounds while trying to avoid The Blob, they must then connect with the nearest blob and continue to play.
- The last two players left outside of The Blob become the first blob for the next round.

Variation(s)

- If everyone is playing safely, the blob can stay connected and continue to grow bigger and bigger until all the players are tagged. Challenge the group to stay together when they move.
- If linking elbows is too challenging, consider linking hands.

Bob the Bunny

→ *Supports Self-Management, Decision-Making, Problem-Solving*

 **GROUP SIZE**
10+ players

 **AGE GROUP**
K–2nd

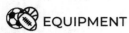 **EQUIPMENT**
Small object or ball, preferably a toy bunny

 TIME
5–10 minutes

Before You Start

- Introduce the players to Bob the Bunny, a small object or ball, preferably a toy bunny.
- Gather the group of players in a circle. Have players place their hands behind their backs.
- Choose one player to be in the middle.

How to Play

- The player in the middle is trying to guess who on the outside of the circle is holding the bunny.
- To begin, the player in the middle closes his or her eyes while the group begins chanting in rhythm, "Bob the Bunny, Bob, Bob, the Bunny!"
- As the players are chanting, start passing the bunny around the circle, keeping the bunny behind everyone's backs.
- Once the bunny is in motion, the player in the middle opens his or her eyes and gets three tries to guess who is holding the bunny. The group is still chanting and passing the bunny.

- If the player in the middle guesses correctly he or she changes places with the player caught holding the bunny.
- If the player in the middle does not guess correctly within three tries he or she becomes part of the circle and a new player is chosen to go in the middle.

Variation(s)

- Player in the middle chooses how many times to chant "Bob the Bunny" keeping his or her eyes closed the whole time.
- Play with multiple bunnies.

Cookie Jar

→ *Supports Self-Management, Decision-Making*

 GROUP SIZE
10+ players

 AGE GROUP
K–2nd

 EQUIPMENT
Cones, if needed for boundaries

 TIME
5–10 minutes

Set-Up

Set up a rectangular play area with enough space in between for the group to run.

Before You Start

- Demonstrate safe and gentle tagging (butterfly tags) and appropriate tagging areas (arms, back, and shoulders).
- Line up players shoulder to shoulder along one of the boundary lines, making sure there is adequate space for the players to spread out.
- Practice the verbal cues so the whole group asks, "Cookie Monster, Cookie Monster, are you hungry?" in unison.
- Review boundaries and consequences for going out of bounds.
- Choose a Cookie Monster (or be the Cookie Monster for the first round). Explain that everyone else is a cookie. It is almost lunchtime and the monster may be hungry.

How to Play

- The players ask, "Cookie Monster, Cookie Monster, are you hungry?"
- If the reply is "no," the player must remain in place and ask again until the reply is "yes."
- If the reply is "yes," the player must try to run across the play area without getting tagged by the Cookie Monster.
- If tagged, players become one of the Cookie Monster's helpers for future rounds.
- Once all players have reached the safety of the other side, the next round begins in the same way.

Variation(s)

- Pick a couple of players to be the Cookie Monster.
- Modify for older kids who may not relate to Cookie Monster with "Boogie Monster."

Elbow Tag

→ *Supports Self-Management, Decision-Making*

 **GROUP SIZE**
20–30 players

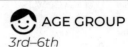 **AGE GROUP**
3rd–6th

 **EQUIPMENT**
No equipment needed

 TIME
10 minutes

Set Up

Designate a playing area large enough to run in.

Before You Start

- Divide the group into partners.
- Partners should link arms at the elbows and have their free hand on their hips.
- Ask for two volunteers. Assign one of them to be It and the other to be the Runner.
- Demonstrate safe tagging (gentle tags) and appropriate tagging areas (arms, back, and shoulders).
- Have the players practice how to detach, and explain who becomes the Runner and who stays linked at the elbow.

How to Play

- The player who is It must try to tag the Runner.
- The Runner must find a pair of players and link arms at the elbow with one of them.

     Why Play Works: Big Changes Start Small

- The player on the other side of that pair detaches and is now the new Runner being chased by the It player.
- The new Runner must then find another pair with whom to attach, in turn detaching another player.
- If the Runner gets tagged before he or she can find someone with whom to link elbows, the Runner then becomes It and chases the other player.
- The Runner must link to another pair within five seconds.

Variation(s)

- The leader says "Switch" and the Runner becomes It.
- Let both the runner and the tagger link elbows, so both have a chance to change and more people get to play.

Four Square

→ *Supports Self-Management, Positive Relationships, Problem-Solving*

 **GROUP SIZE**
4+ players

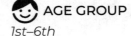 **AGE GROUP**
1st–6th

 **EQUIPMENT**
1 rubber playground ball

 TIME
10 minutes

Set Up

- Draw a Four-Square court: 10-by-10-foot square, divided into four smaller squares of 5-by-5 feet each.
- Clockwise, label the squares with chalk: 1, 2, 3, 4.

Before You Start

- Explain that the object of the game is to hit the ball into another player's square.
- Demonstrate what flat underhand hits look like (open palms).
- Explain that if there is a disagreement about a play, 1 round of Rock, Paper, Scissors resolves the conflict.

How to Play

- The game begins when the player in square 1 serves the ball.
- To serve, the player bounces the ball, then hits it underhand into another player's square.
- The receiver lets the ball bounce once before hitting it into another player's square.

- Play continues until the ball bounces out of bounds, bounces twice before it is returned, is not allowed to bounce, or bounces on a line.
- The player who causes any of these goes to the end of the line, and a new player enters into square 4.
- When a square is left open, the person in the front advances to the next square, and the remaining players close the gap. For example, if square 1 is open, the player in square 2 would move to 1, square 3 moves to 2, and so on. New players always enter the game in square 4.

Variation(s)

- Categories. The replacement player names any category they want: animals, colors, sports, counting by 5s, and so on. Players must call out something that falls under that category when the ball comes to them. If there's a repeat or a player can't think of anything fast enough he or she goes to the end of the line. All of the normal rules still apply.
- Example: The server announces "Colors! Purple." The next player calls out "blue" and so on.

Gaga Ball

→ *Supports Self-Management, Social Awareness/Empathy, Decision-Making*

 GROUP SIZE
4+ players

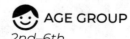 **AGE GROUP**
2nd–6th

 EQUIPMENT
Dodge balls

 TIME
5–15 minutes

Set Up

Define an appropriate play space with clear boundaries. You will need enough space for players to move around trying to hit the ball or avoid a bouncing ball.

Before You Start

- Demonstrate paddle hands and how to hit the ball with an open hand.
- Demonstrate tagging with the ball from the knee down.

How to Play

- The object of the game is to be the last person left in the play area.
- All players start by standing on the boundary of the play area.
- One designated player walks to the center and throws the ball in the air.
- Players count three bounces before they run in and can try to hit the ball with their paddle hands.

- If a player hits the ball, he or she cannot touch it again until the ball hits something else—either another player hits it, the ball tags another player, or the ball touches a wall.
- If a player gets tagged by the ball below the knee, he or she becomes a part of the boundary and help keep the ball in the area.
- The game is over when there is one player left or time runs out.

Variation(s)

- Use multiple balls.
- Put tables/desks on their side and create a hexagon or an octagon.

Giants, Wizards, and Elves

→ *Supports Positive Relationships, Problem-Solving, Teamwork*

 **GROUP SIZE**
10–30 players

 **AGE GROUP**
3rd–6th

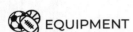 **EQUIPMENT**
Cones or chalk, if needed for boundaries

 TIME
20 minutes or more

Set Up

- Define the playing area with cones in a rectangular shape.
- Divide the group into two teams.

Before You Start

- Demonstrate the movement and sound for each character:
  - The giants stand with hands raised overhead and make the sound "Aaargh!"
  - The wizards stand with one arm extended forward as if they are holding a wand and makes the sound "Hissssss!"
- The elves squat down, put their hands around their ears, and make the sound "Hehehehehe!"
- Have the whole group practice each of the characters' movement and sound.
- Explain which character wins in a stand-off: giant over wizard, wizard over elf, and elf over giant.
- Demonstrate safe and gentle tagging (butterfly tags) and appropriate tagging areas (arms, back, and shoulders).

How to Play

- Each team huddles up on its side and chooses a first and second character.
- Each team moves to the middle line, walking shoulder-to-shoulder.
- Then the leader calls out, "One, two, three! What's it gonna be?"
- Teams flash their first choice.
- The team that flashes the dominant character chases the other team back to its line, trying to tag as many players as possible before they get to their line
- Anyone tagged becomes part of the opposite team.
- If both teams choose the same first choice, the teams wait for the leader to again call out the signal, and the teams flash their second choice. If they choose the same second choice, the teams regroup and pick two new choices.
- Play continues until all players are on the same team.

Variation(s)

- Use three different objects, movements, and sounds. Possible options include Lions, Tigers, and Bears; or Rock, Paper, and Scissors.

Hula Hoop Challenge

→ *Supports Positive Relationships, Problem-Solving, Teamwork*

 GROUP SIZE
10–30 players

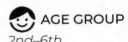 **AGE GROUP**
2nd–6th

 **EQUIPMENT**
1–2 hula hoops

 TIME
5–10 minutes

Set Up

- The group forms a circle, holding hands.
- Demonstrate how to get your body through the hula hoop while staying connected in the circle, still holding hands.

Before You Start

- Two players unclasp their hands so you can place the hula hoop between them. Then they grasp hands again, with the hoop between them, and their hands through the hoop.

How to Play

- The object of the game is to get the hula hoop all the way around the circle without anyone letting go of their teammates' hands.
- Encourage the group to cheer each other on.
- Once the task is accomplished, have the group discuss successes and challenges and try again if time permits.

Variation(s)

- Time the group to see how quickly the players can do the activity.
- Play with eyes shut.
- Divide the group in two circles and have them compete.

Hungry Fox

→ *Supports Self-Management, Decision-Making, Teamwork*

 **GROUP SIZE**
7–30 players

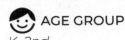 **AGE GROUP**
K–2nd

 **EQUIPMENT**
Chalk, cones

 TIME
10–20 minutes

Set Up

Designate a large rectangular play area with clear boundaries and enough room for children to skip, jog, or run. On one end of the rectangle have a line of chalk or cones that will be the designated safe zone.

Before You Start

- Demonstrate safe and gentle tagging (butterfly tags) and appropriate tagging areas (arms, back, and shoulders).
- Ask players to practice butterfly tagging on their own upper back, shoulders, and arms so they know where safe touch is.
- Ask players: "Do we hit, grab, push, or pull when using butterfly tags?" Make sure all answers to the questions are "no."
- Practice with the players starting the game. Players must ask "Hungry Fox, Hungry Fox, what time is it?"
- Demonstrate what happens when players get tagged. Tagged players freeze and become the Hungry Fox's helpers.
- Show the players the safe line that they need to pass where the Hungry Fox cannot tag them.

Why Play Works: Big Changes Start Small

- Review the boundaries, the safe zone, and the consequence for going outside them (players become a Hungry Fox helper).

How to Play

- The object of the game is to avoid being tagged by the Hungry Fox.
- Players stand shoulder to shoulder on the starting line in the safe zone.
- One player or the leader begins the game in the middle of the boundaries as the Hungry Fox.
- Players ask, "Hungry Fox, Hungry Fox, what time is it?"
- Whatever time (from 1 o'clock to 12 o'clock) the Hungry Fox says, is the number of steps players take out of the safe zone, toward the fox.
- If the Hungry Fox says "It's lunchtime" players must run back to their safe zone without getting tagged.
- Tagged players become one of Hungry Fox's helpers and tag the other players.
- The last player untagged in the safe zone becomes the Hungry Fox for the next round!

Mid-Game Questions

[Use this as an opportunity to reteach safe tagging.]

- Where do we tag our classmates?
- How are we tagging our classmates, using what kind of light fingers do we use?

Variation(s)

- Modify movement and speed of play, especially if a large group is playing. Hop like bunnies, skip, zombie walk, tiptoe, and so on. Younger players often do better with hops than steps.
- To increase safety, when the first person is tagged, he or she becomes the new Hungry Fox for the next round.

I Love My Neighbor

→ *Supports Positive Relationships, Social Awareness/Empathy*

 **GROUP SIZE**
5+ players

 **AGE GROUP**
K–5th

 **EQUIPMENT**
One less chair, cone, or place marker than the participants playing

 TIME
10 minutes

Set Up

Position chairs, cones, or place markers to form a circle.

Before You Start

- Prompt players to think about what they will say if they get to be in the middle (activities they like to do, foods they like to eat, movies they like to watch, and so on).
- Briefly talk about the need for awareness of others (being aware of your surroundings and other people moving in the same space) and review Rock, Paper, Scissors, in case there is a tie.

How to Play

- Players stand in a circle where the cone/place marker marks their spot. One player will not have a cone. That person stands in the center of the circle.

- The player standing in the center begins the game by saying, "I love my neighbor who . . ." The player completes the sentence with a fact about themselves. For example, "I love my neighbor who likes to play basketball!" or "I love my neighbor who has brothers and sisters!" The sentence can be anything that the player likes, but must be true for that person.
- Then all players on the circle who have that in common leave their spot and run to any empty spot that is not right next to them.
- The last player who cannot find an open spot changes places with the person in the center and begins a new round of the game by saying, "I love my neighbor who . . ."

Knockout

→ *Supports Self-Management*

 **GROUP SIZE**
5–15 players

 **AGE GROUP**
3rd–6th

 **EQUIPMENT**
2 basketballs, basketball hoop, cone

 TIME
10–15 minutes

Set Up

Place one cone a few feet behind the foul line, facing the basket.

Before You Start

- Review how to shoot the basketball.
- Review start and stop signals.

How to Play

- Players form one line at the cone.
- The first two players in line start with a ball.
- The object of the game is for the player who gets to the court second to score before the player who was already there.
- On the start signal, Player 1 proceeds to the foul line and takes his or her first shot.
  - As soon as Player 1 attempts his or her first shot, Player 2 can shoot from the foul line.
  - If players miss their first shot from the foul line, they can rebound and shoot from anywhere on the court. Players continue to shoot until one of them makes a basket.

- Both players are trying to be the first to make a basket.
- If Player 2 makes a basket before Player 1, Player 1 is knocked out.
  - Both players pass their balls to the front of the line.
  - Player 2 returns to the end of the line.
  - Player 1 waits until the next game.
- If Player 1 makes a basket before Player 2, Player 2 continues to shoot.
  - Player 1, passes the ball to the first person in line and goes to the end of the line.
  - The next player, Player 3, shoots from the foul line, now trying to make a shot before Player 2.
- This rotation continues until there is only one player left.
- Once players score or are knocked out, they pass the ball to the next person in line as quickly as possible. Passing quickly allows the next shooter the greatest chance of eliminating another player.
- Players may not touch the other player's ball at any time.

Land, Sea, Air

→ *Supports Decision-Making*

 **GROUP SIZE**
4–60 players

 **AGE GROUP**
K–6th

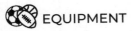 **EQUIPMENT**
A line or an imaginary line

 TIME
1–10 minutes

Set Up

Either mark a line on the floor or just create a space where players can stand with enough space between them so they don't knock into each other.

Before You Start

For younger players, this game benefits from a quick, playful story. Once you understand how to play this game, think of a story that will help you bring this game to life for your players.

How to Play

- The leader calls out commands, such as "land," "air," "sea," in no particular order.
- Players must do what the commands represent.
- When the leader calls "sea," the players jump over the line into the sea.

- When the leader calls "air," the players jump straight up and land back in the same spot (not crossing over into the other area).
- When the leader calls a command that matches the players' position, the players remain standing on the ground—doing nothing. Example: calling out "land" when the players are all standing on land already.
- The leader's goal is to confuse the players by mixing up all the commands in any order the leader chooses.
- When a player makes a mistake, they do a fun task to get back into the game. Examples: five seconds of dancing, telling yourself "I'm awesome" while fist-pumping up in the air, getting a High Five from the leader, or anything else you want. Be creative!

Mid-Game Questions

- What do you need to do to last as long as possible in this game?

Closing Questions

- What kind of skills are we practicing in this game?
- When would be a good time to play this game and why?

Variation(s)

- The leader speeds up the command delivery.
- The group plays until there is one player left, then the last one standing becomes the leader of the next round.

- The leader can make up a variety of commands, based on the age and ability of the players. Examples:
  - Bridge—one foot in the land, and one foot in the sea
  - Tornado—spin in a circle one time
  - Swimmer—jump into the sea and do a swimmer's crawl arm movement
  - Farmer—jump onto land pretend to hoe
  - Bird—jump into air with arms outstretched like a bird
- The leader could use this game as a transition for moving students into the next classroom activity: the players who make a wrong movement are then last to get a drink, get a snack, start homework, and so on.

Mountains and Valleys

→ *Supports Self-Management, Social Awareness/Empathy, Decision-Making, Teamwork*

 GROUP SIZE
10–30 players

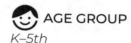 **AGE GROUP**
K–5th

 EQUIPMENT
20–30 cones

 TIME
5–10 minutes

Set Up

Place cones randomly inside the boundaries of the game. Some cones should be right-side-up. Some cones should be upside-down or on their side.

Before You Start

- Remind players to be careful not to run into each other.
- Remind players that the game begins and ends with the sound of your whistle.

How to Play

- Divide players into two teams: the Mountains and the Valleys.
- The Mountain Team turns cones into mountains by turning them right-side-up.
- The Valley Team turns cones into valleys by turning them upside-down.

- Cones must be moved gently with hands only. Feet should never touch the cones.
- Play continues for about one minute, and then the leader blows a whistle.
- Count how many cones are Mountains and how many are Valleys.
- After a few rounds, teams switch roles.

Variation(s)

- When playing inside, have players place the cones on top of desks, chairs, and tables.

Night at the Museum

→ *Supports Self-Management, Decision-Making*

 **GROUP SIZE**
5+ players

 **AGE GROUP**
K–6th

EQUIPMENT
Cones

 TIME
10–15 minutes

Set Up

Clear the play space of obstacles and mark clear boundaries.

Before You Start

- Talk to players about statues:
    - They don't move.
    - They don't touch each other.
    - They don't make noise.
    - But we all know they come alive and move around the museum at night, right?
- Remind players to be safe and be aware of where their friends are around them.
- Have players practice appropriate statue poses.
- Explain that the night guard will hold a pretend flashlight and look for moving statues (a cone, marker, anything they can pretend is a flashlight).

How to Play

- The object of the game is to move without letting the night guard see you. On the start word, all players become a statue and can't let the night guard catch them moving.
- The night guard will move slowly around the room, pointing his or her flashlight at the statues. If the night guard shines the flashlight on a player and that player moves or laughs, he or she becomes a night guard.
- If playing this indoors/in a classroom, encourage players to be sneaky when they're moving around. You do not want the night guard to hear you moving!

Variation(s)

- For older players, this game can be combined with other games, such as silent ball, for an added challenge.

One Fish, Two Fish, Red Fish, Blue Fish

→ *Supports Self-Management, Positive Relationships, Problem-Solving, Teamwork*

 GROUP SIZE
10–35 players

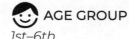 **AGE GROUP**
1st–6th

 EQUIPMENT
Small object like a stuffed animal fish

 TIME
10–15 minutes

Set Up

Create a visible starting line.

Before You Start

- Players line up on the starting line.
- The leader places an object a good distance from the starting line—at least 15 feet or more.

How to Play

- The object of the game is for the players to work as a team to get the object back to the starting line without the leader guessing who has it.
- The leader stands behind the object facing the players.
- The leader turns with his or her back to the players and says, "One Fish, Two Fish, Red Fish, Blue Fish."
- Players move while the leader is saying the phrase.

- When the leader finishes ". . . Blue Fish," the leader turns around and all the players freeze.
- If anyone is still moving when the leader turns around, the whole group must go back to the starting line.
- If no players are caught moving, the leader turns around again and says "One Fish, Two Fish, Red Fish, Blue Fish," and the players can move closer to the object.
- Once the players get close enough for one of them to take the object, all players pretend they have it, with their hands behind their backs.
- Players still may only move during the phrase—now going backward—but once the object has been taken, the leader takes three guesses during each freeze, trying to find out who has it.
- If the leader guesses correctly, the object is returned, and the players start over back at the starting line.
- If the leader guesses incorrectly, he or she turns around, says the phrase, and the players keep moving toward the finish line.
- This play rotation continues until either the object holder is correctly identified, or the group gets the object back to the safety line and a new round begins.

Variation(s)

- Set a minimum number of players who must touch the object before it crosses the line.
- Require that all students touch the object at least once before it crosses the line.
- Increase the distance between the object and the starting line.

Over Under

→ *Supports Positive Relationships, Social Awareness/Empathy, Decision-Making, Problem Solving*

 GROUP SIZE
10–30 players

 AGE GROUP
2nd–5th

 EQUIPMENT
1 ball per team (teams of 8–10 players)

 **TIME**
10 minutes

Set Up

Designate a start and finish line.

Before You Start

- Have players line up behind each other in groups of 8 to 10, spreading out an arm's length apart.
- Demonstrate how to pass the ball over someone's head then under and through someone's legs.
- Give the player in front of the line a ball.

How to Play

- The object of the game is for players to pass back the ball either over their head or under their legs, alternating methods with each person.
- When the last person in line gets the ball, he or she goes to the front of the line and starts passing the ball back again.

- The line should be moving forward with each person going to the front of the line.
- Play until the players reach a finishing point or until a specific number of turns.

Variation(s)

- Have players shut their eyes while they are passing and receiving.
- Play with a basketball where the players must take a shot at a basket before returning to the front of the line.
- Add dribbling challenges such as left or right hand only or pivoting before passing.
- Play with a soccer ball with similar challenges.
- Vary the way players move from the back to the front of the line.

Poop Deck

→ *Supports Self-Management, Problem-Solving*

 GROUP SIZE
10+ players

 EQUIPMENT
Chalk

 **AGE GROUP**
K–2nd

 TIME
5–10 minutes

Set Up

- Create a large rectangle split into three equal sections using chalk or cones.
- Designate or label the sections: Poop Deck, Quarter Deck, and Main Deck.

Before You Start

- Line players up on the sideline. Make sure all players have room to move safely between the decks.
- Make sure all players know where each deck is located.
- Review the importance of awareness and honesty.

How to Play

- Players line up with their toes behind the sideline.
- The Caller stands at the end line and shouts either "Poop Deck!" or "Quarter Deck!" or "Main Deck!"
- All players run to the called area.

- The last player to cross over the line sings the Awesome Song and gets back into the game.
- The Caller judges whether a player did not make it.

Variation(s)

- The last player to cross over the line becomes a Caller's assistant, calling together until the next round.
- The last player in becomes the new Caller for the next round before rejoining the other players.
- Create new commands, incorporating other skills like walking, skipping, hopping.

Ro-Sham-Bo Rockstar

→ *Supports Positive Relationships*

 **GROUP SIZE**
10–100 players

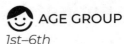 **AGE GROUP**
1st–6th

 **EQUIPMENT**
No equipment needed

 TIME
10 minutes

Set Up

Define the boundaries of the play space.

Before You Start

Review the rules to Ro-Sham-Bo (also known as Rock, Paper, Scissors).

How to Play

- Divide players into pairs.
- Players introduce themselves to each other.
- Partners play a round of Ro-Sham-Bo (or enough rounds to break a tie).
- The unsuccessful partner becomes the winner's fan.
- The fan follows the winning partner, cheering and supporting the partner.
- The winner moves on to play another winning player, with the fans behind the winners, cheering them on.

- Each round, the winner advances to play again, collecting fans.
- The game continues until the last round of two players, each with a group of fans.
- The winner of this last round is the Ro-Sham-Bo Rockstar.

Sequence Touch

→ Supports Self-Management

 **GROUP SIZE**
5–60 players

 **AGE GROUP**
K–5th

 **EQUIPMENT**
Optional cones, chalk, line

 TIME
1–5 minutes

Set Up

Create a home base using cones, chalk, or an imaginary space where players will always start and finish each task.

Before You Start

- Designate an area with objects that many players can run to and tag (basketball hoop, fence, grass, slide, jungle gym).
- Review ways to be safe while running:
  - Demonstrate how to avoid others when running toward the object to tag.
  - Remind players to keep their heads up.
  - Players do not have to always go straight. They can move side to side to avoid other players.
- Show players where the return location is after they tag all of the objects.

How to Play

- The object of the game is for players to remember and tag all of the objects that are listed as quickly as they can and return to the designated area (home base).
- When the leader says the start word, everyone must go tag the objects before returning to the same spot within 10 seconds. Objects will be based on whatever is available in the location.
- Helpful tip: have players repeat the instructions back to you before you say the start word.

Variation(s)

- Use as a Transition Activity: choose a style of moving appropriate for your space (walking, tiptoeing) and change the final destination ("your desk with your math book out").
- Don't have a time limit.
- Have players touch the objects with different parts of their bodies.
- Have players touch a category of object ("something red that is not clothing").
- Have players perform an action ("give two High Fives," "give a double High Five to someone wearing red").
- Modify the movements. Players could skip, hop, or run like an animal.
- Add basketballs or soccer balls to make this game a great skill-building activity for dribbling.

Shipwreck

→ *Supports Self-Management, Social Awareness/Empathy*

 **GROUP SIZE**
5+ players

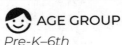 **AGE GROUP**
Pre-K–6th

 **EQUIPMENT**
Cones or chalk, if needed for boundaries

 TIME
5+ minutes

Set Up

- Designate an appropriate play area with clear boundaries: outside, in a gym, or in a classroom.

Before You Start

- Players line up on a clearly marked line in the middle of the playing area.
- Make sure everyone knows the commands and understands the activity they prompt.
- Start with a few commands and increase the number of commands you use as players are able to remember them.
- The object of the game is to be the last crew member standing.
- The leader explains that he or she is the captain of the ship and will give commands to the crew.
- The crew is sailing treacherous seas and must work together and follow the captain's commands to survive.

- If crew members do not follow the commands correctly or is the last to follow the command, they must go to the brig (waiting area).

How to Play

- The captain calls out commands, and the crew must obey or be thrown in the brig.
  - **Roll call.** The crew lines up at the midline of the playing area, feet together, toes on the line, salute, and say, "Aye-aye, Captain!" The crew holds the salute until the captain salutes and says, "At ease."
  - **Crow's nest.** Players act as if they're climbing up a ladder to the crow's nest, at the top of the main mast, to serve as lookouts.
  - **Swab the deck.** Players act like they're mopping the deck while chanting, "Swab, swab, swab the deck!"
  - **Shark attack.** The Captain becomes a shark and tries to tag the crew. Those tagged go to the brig.
  - **Break time.** Active crew members run to the brig and tag as many people as possible. Those who are tagged come back in and play. Make sure everyone gets let out of the brig during break time.
  - **Sailor overboard.** Crew members get into groups of three. Two crew members grab hands forming a life raft and the third gets into the middle while acting out using a spy-glass to find the sailor in the water.
  - **Drop anchor.** Crew members lie on their backs with legs up and act like an anchor.

- **Pirate crew.** Crew members close one eye, put up a hook finger, hobble around like they have a peg leg, and say "Aaargh!"
- **Row to shore.** Crew members make lines of four. Players act as if they are rowing, while singing "Row, Row, Row Your Boat."
- **Chow time.** Five crew members make a small circle. All of them bend slightly toward the center, then mime eating handfuls of food while saying, "Um num num num num!!!"
- Players will inevitably be without a group on different rounds. You can either send them to the brig to perform a designated exercise (jumping jacks, pushups, star jumps), have them become swimmers who swim around the room until they hear the next direction, or wait until break time when another player will rescue them with a High Five.

Variation(s)

- Create and add new rules, especially ones that require players to form groups of two, three, four, five, and more!
- For newer players, pick two or three rules on which to focus.

Sprout Ball

→ *Supports Self-Management, Social Awareness/Empathy*

 GROUP SIZE
5–30 players

 **AGE GROUP**
2nd–6th

 **EQUIPMENT**
Soft playground balls

 TIME
5–15 minutes

Set Up

Set up an appropriate boundary for the play area.

Before You Start

- Review appropriate places to hit with the dodgeball (below the waist or it doesn't count) and dodgeball throwing safety (throw gently). This game can also be played as Sprout Tag without using balls.

How to Play

- The players start at the edges of the boundaries in their own space.
- The object of the game is to be the last player standing.
- The ball is thrown into the air and bounces three times. On the third bounce the players can leave their spot and try to pick up the ball.
- Once players grab the ball, they can only take three steps and can only hold onto the ball for five seconds.

- The player with the ball throws at any player, trying to tag him or her from the waist down.
- If the other player is tagged, he or she become a "seed" by crouching down or taking a knee. Students with limited mobility can put their hands on their knees or use another adaptation.
- If the player is not tagged but catches the ball, the player who threw the ball becomes a seed instead.
- Seeds should point at the player who tagged him or her and keep an eye on this player.
- Seeds can "sprout" up and keep playing when the person who tagged him or her is tagged.
- The game is over when all of the players have been tagged by the same player or time runs out.

Variation(s)

- Use multiple balls. Or, play Sprout Tag without any balls.
- Once players have been tagged and are sitting down, if a ball comes close enough to grab, they can try to free themselves by throwing the ball at standing players.

Steal the Bacon

→ *Supports Decision-Making, Teamwork*

 GROUP SIZE
10+ players

 AGE GROUP
3rd–6th

EQUIPMENT
Bean bags

 TIME
10–15 minutes

Set Up

- Designate a play area with clear boundaries and a goal line for each team.
- Play area can be indoors or outdoors such as a basketball court, field, or other large rectangular area.

Before You Start

- Demonstrate safe and gentle tagging (butterfly tags) and appropriate tagging areas (arms, back, and shoulders).
- Check for understanding by having participants repeat the rules back to you.
- Keep in mind that younger grade levels may have difficulty remembering their numbers.

How to Play

- Divide participants into two to four teams, depending on group size.

- Give each player a number, say 1 to 5; assign the same numbers, 1 to 5, to the other team.
- Place the bacon (bean bag or other small item) in the middle of the playing area.
- The leader calls out a number, and each player with that number runs to pick up the bacon.
- The player who gets the bacon first, runs back to his or her goal line, while the opposing player tries to tag his player before he or she brings home the bacon.
- The round ends once a player with the bacon is tagged or reaches the goal line.
- At the end of the round, each player gives the other player a High Five before returning back to their respective team.

Variation(s)

- Use addition/subtraction, multiplication/division to call out the numbers, such as the players with the number that is equal to two plus three.
- Call more than one number at a time, and/or require players to pass the bacon once before they score.
- Place two pieces of bacon in a hula hoop in the center and make sure teams know which ball and which goal is theirs.
- Soccer style. Use a soccer ball as the bacon. The objective is to be the first team to kick the ball into a goal at the finish line. The leader can use one ball or one ball for each team.
- Basketball style. Use a basketball ball as the bacon. The objective is to be the first team to score a basket in a nearby hoop. The leader can use one ball or one ball for each team.

Superstar

→ *Supports Self-Management, Positive Relationships, Social Awareness/Empathy, Teamwork*

 GROUP SIZE
6–30 players

 AGE GROUP
2nd+

EQUIPMENT
None

 TIME
10–15 minutes

Set Up

None.

Before You Start

- Have the whole group gather in a circle.
- Divide players into pairs.
- Demonstrate with a volunteer examples of commonalities that meet the criteria.
  - "I wouldn't tell my partner that I have brown hair because they can see that. I wouldn't say that I am in elementary school because my partner already knows that. I might say, my favorite food is pizza. What's yours? What do you like to do in your spare time?"

How to Play

- Each group will have one to two minutes to find out how many things the group members have in common that:

- They didn't already know and
- Are not visible
- When the time is up have players get into a circle, standing next to their partner.
- One by one, each pair will share one thing both have in common.
- After sharing this commonality, if others in the group also share that commonality they all will put their hands in the air, lunge forward, and yell "SUPERSTAR!"
- The next pair then shares a commonality and the process continues until all pairs have shared.

Variation(s)

- Have players switch partners and do a round where they have to find out what they have in common around a specific topic (sports, school, and so on).
- Have players do a round where they can't speak and can only act out ideas.

Switch

→ *Supports Self-Management*

 **GROUP SIZE**
5–30 players

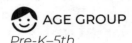 **AGE GROUP**
Pre-K–5th

 **EQUIPMENT**
5 cones

 TIME
10 minutes

Set Up

Create a square with four cones on each corner and one in the middle of the square. You can also use a four square court, pointing out the four corners and the center intersection.

Before You Start

Review how to play Rock, Paper, Scissors.

How to Play

- Players line up close to the playing area.
- The first five players in line each stand at a cone (at each corner and in the middle).
- Play begins when the player in the middle yells "Switch."
- All five players, including the player in the middle, walk quickly to find a new corner cone to occupy. Players may not stay at their cone or return to the same cone.
- If two players come to a cone at the same time, they use Rock, Paper, Scissors to determine who will stay at the cone.

- If a player does not get to a corner cone, he or she returns to the game line.
- The next player in the line goes to the middle cone and begins the next round.

Variation(s)

- Add cones—say halfway between the corners—to make a bigger play area for more than five players.
- Use four different colored hula hoops. Have the player in the middle call out a color, the caller runs to that color hula hoop. All other players have to switch hula hoops but cannot run to the color that was called out.
- Have players pick a different way to move each round (tip toes, bunny hop, etc.).

Three Lines Basketball

→ *Supports Self-Management, Decision-Making, Teamwork*

 **GROUP SIZE**
10+ players

 AGE GROUP
3rd–6th

 **EQUIPMENT**
Basketball, cones for lines

 TIME
10–15 minutes

Set Up

Place three cones on the center line of a basketball court.

Before You Start

- Demonstrate how to dribble with one hand.
- Explain and demonstrate traveling (taking more than two steps without dribbling).
- Explain and demonstrate passing techniques (bounce and chest passes).
- Demonstrate shooting techniques.
- Demonstrate how to defend another player without making contact, shuffling one's feet with arms up or wide.
- Explain that the ball changes teams after going out of bounds.

How to Play

- Players stand in three single-file lines, one behind each cone.

- The first player in each line steps onto the court to form a team of three (starting as defense).
- The second player in each line steps onto the other side of the court to form another team of three (starting as offense).
- The two teams play a round of half-court basketball, each trying to score a basket before the other team.
- When a point is scored, the scoring team stays on the court as the defenders and the next three in line step on the court as a team. This oncoming team plays offense.
- The team that did not score returns to the end of the lines.
- If a point is not scored after a set time, players waiting in line count down from 10.
- If neither team has scored a point by the end of the count-down, both teams leave the court and join their respective lines; two new teams step onto the court.
- If a team wins three times in a row, it earns three claps and returns to the end of the lines.

Variation(s)

- Players cannot dribble. In order to move the ball, they must pass.
- When players on defense rebound the ball, they must pass it one time before they can shoot the ball.
- Each player on a team must touch the ball a certain number of times before a team can shoot.

Toxic Waste Dump

→ *Supports Positive Relationships, Social Awareness/Empathy, Problem-Solving, Teamwork*

 **GROUP SIZE**
10–30 players

 **AGE GROUP**
3rd–6th

 **EQUIPMENT**
Cardboard, jump rope, paper, carpet squares, or anything that players can easily stand on and carry

 **TIME**
10 minutes or more

Set Up

- Make a clearly marked start and finish line.
- Have all materials set out and ready for use.

Before You Start

- The team should come up with a strategy on how to get all of their teammates across the playing area safely without stepping in toxic sludge.
- Brainstorm strategies and give examples if needed.

How to Play

- The object of the game is to get all players from one side of the playing area to the other side without touching the toxic sludge.

- Players can only be in the toxic sludge if they are standing on an item provided.
- If players step off and into the sludge, they must return to the other side of town.
- If an item is placed into the toxic sludge without being constantly touched by a player, it is lost and the whole team must return back to the other side of town.

Variation(s)

- Everyone works together to race against a clock.
- Split the group into teams and see which team can complete the task first.
- Choose the amount of items based on the experience level of the group.
- Players figure out their plan before they start then remain silent during the game.
- Randomly blindfold or silence a few members of the group.

Triangle Tag

→ Supports Self-Management, Positive Relationships, Social Awareness/Empathy, Decision-Making, Problem-Solving, Teamwork

---

 **GROUP SIZE**
4–80 players

 **AGE GROUP**
2nd–5th

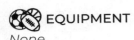 **EQUIPMENT**
None

 TIME
5 minutes

Set Up

Designate a clear playing area.

Before You Start

- Divide players into groups of four with three of the four holding hands in a triangle.
- Help players choose one of the three players holding hands to be the Runner, the person to be tagged.
- Demonstrate safe and gentle tagging (butterfly tags) and appropriate tagging areas (arms, back, and shoulders).

How to Play

- The player outside the circle is the Tagger, trying to tag the Runner.

- The other two players holding hands in the triangle will help to protect the designated Runner by moving in different directions.
- The tagger cannot go inside, over, or under the triangle, and cannot lean on the arms of the players holding hands.
- Once the Tagger has tagged the Runner or time runs out, the positions change.
- Keep an eye on the play and make sure groups are changing positions.

Ultimate Kickball

→ *Supports Positive Relationships, Decision-Making, Teamwork*

 **GROUP SIZE**
10+ players

 **AGE GROUP**
1st–4th

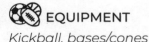 **EQUIPMENT**
Kickball, bases/cones

 **TIME**
15–20 minutes

Set Up

- This game can be played on a regular kickball field or by using four cones for bases in a large area.
- Bases should be large enough to fit multiple players.

Before You Start

- Remind players to play in a position (spread out) and to call the ball.
- Encourage passing the ball by throwing it to teammates rather than running it.
- Remind players to tag softly with the ball.
- Review the order of the bases and running in a counter-clockwise direction.

How to Play

- Divide the group into two teams: a kicking team and a fielding team.

- The pitcher controls play of the game. Play begins when the ball is rolled to the kicker, and play stops when the pitcher has the ball.
- The pitcher will roll the ball to home base and the kicker.
- The kicker will kick the ball and run the bases in order. One point is scored for each runner that rounds all bases and reaches home base safely.
- There are no foul balls.
- Players can kick the ball backward only if there is a backstop or wall behind home plate.
- There can be more than one runner on a base at any time.
- Runners may choose to stay on one base if it is unsafe to run.
- Runners can pass each other at any time.
- Runners must return to the previous base if the pitcher has the ball before they are halfway to the next base.
- Runners cannot continue running the bases and should return to their team if their fly ball is caught before it bounces or if they are tagged while not on a base.
- Teams switch after everyone on the kicking team has kicked once.

Variation(s)

Note: this version of kickball works well because it allows the advanced players to run fast through the bases and it allows beginners to take their time and learn the game.

Whistle Mixer

→ *Supports Social Awareness/Empathy*

 **GROUP SIZE**
5+ players

 **AGE GROUP**
Pre-K–6th

 **EQUIPMENT**
Cones or chalk, if needed for boundaries, whistle

 TIME
5 minutes

Set Up

Designate a play area with clear, visible boundaries.

Before You Start

- Players need to be scattered within a playing area. Have them walk around without touching each other. Feel free to have them skip, hop, or jump.
- Have a practice round so players can get the idea before they are put under any pressure.

How to Play

- The leader will blow a whistle a different number of times.
- When the leader blows the whistle, the players must form groups with the same number of players as whistle blows. So if the leader blows the whistle four times, the players must group themselves in groups of four.

- Players can be directed to hold hands or perform a number of physical movements once they form their group.
- Have players who were not able to form with a group step out and do a short activity like jumping jacks or the "I'm Awesome" dance, after which they may rejoin the game.
- For the next round, groups should spread out before regrouping so the same players are not near to each other again.

Variation(s)

- Pre-K: when the leader blows the whistle, players must find a partner as quickly as possible. Remind players to let go of their partner's hand before blowing the whistle again. Repeat, asking them to find a new partner each time.
- You can challenge the more advanced players by requiring them to perform a specific task when the whistle is blown before they can form groups.
- Indoor modifications: instead of using a whistle, clap or snap to reduce the noise indoors.

Who Stole the Cookies?

→ *Supports Positive Relationships, Social Awareness/Empathy*

 **GROUP SIZE**
5+ players

 **AGE GROUP**
Pre-K–1st

 **EQUIPMENT**
1 ball

 TIME
5 minutes

Set Up

None.

Before You Start

- Have the players stand or sit in a circle.
- Practice rolling the ball to players and sitting down after they rolled.
- Practice singing one round of the song.

How to Play

- The Song:
  - Group: Who stole the cookies from the cookie jar? [insert Leader's name] stole the cookies from the cookie jar!
  - Leader: Who me?
  - Group: Yes you!
  - Leader: Couldn't be!
  - Group: Then who?

- The leader will then roll the ball to a player in the circle (saying their name) and sit down.
- After the leader has said the player's name, the group repeats the same song but with the new player responding.
- Continue to roll the ball to everyone in the group and repeat the song for each player.
- The game is over when all the players have had a turn and are sitting in the circle.

Wolves and Bunnies

→ *Supports Positive Relationships, Problem-Solving, Teamwork*

 **GROUP SIZE**
10–50 players

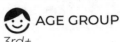 **AGE GROUP**
3rd+

 **EQUIPMENT**
1 ball (playground, dodgeball, football, etc.)

 TIME
10 minutes

Set Up

Set up boundaries. Space should be large enough to accommodate the group with space to move.

Before You Start

Demonstrate safe and gentle tagging (butterfly tags) and appropriate tagging areas (arms, back, and shoulders).

How to Play

- The object of the game is for the wolves to tag all of the bunnies.
- Wolves can only tag bunnies with butterfly tags, not by throwing the ball.
- Bunnies can move all around the play area.
- Wolves can also move all around the play area as long as they do not have the ball in their hands.
- If the wolf has the ball, he or she cannot take any steps and can only pivot on one foot.

- However, wolves can tag bunnies only if they have the ball in their hands.
- Wolves without the ball should strategically move around the play space trying to get closer to the bunnies so that a wolf with the ball can throw it to them when they are close enough to tag the bunnies.
- When a bunny is tagged, they immediately turn into a wolf.
- Play continues until there are only a small number of bunnies left.
- Remaining bunnies will turn into the first set of wolves for the next round.

Variation(s)

- Use different examples of predator and prey.
- Add extra balls or balls of different sizes.

Acknowledgments

I didn't intend to write this book. It wasn't until spring 2020, after the pandemic had shut down all the schools and it was clear that we wouldn't be reopening until the next fall (ha!) that I realized I should reach out to Jossey-Bass to suggest postponing the release of the book I had coauthored with Amanda von Moos on redesigning substitute teaching. It was in that conversation with Riley Harding that the idea for writing the *Playworks Re-Opening Workbook* emerged. *The Re-Opening Workbook* morphed into a free ebook, with the idea that I would do interviews as the schools reopened, providing the basis of *Why Play Works*.

Those initial conversations for the *Re-Opening Workbook* were invaluable in helping me articulate a vision for how play might contribute in this moment. Many thanks to David Bornstein, Brendan Boyle, Marc Brackett, Stuart Brown, Dina Buchbinder, Hedy Chang, Jennette Claassen, Ann Cooper, Danyel Crutcher, Scott Doorley, Cynthia Gentry, Peter Gray, Kathy Hirsh-Pasek, Jessica Hoffmann, Lisa Kay Solomon, Rebecca London, Aleta Margolis, Will Massey, Laura McBain, Susan McKay, Ellen Moir, Constance Moore,

Eileen Pedersen, Kate Rancourt, Ariel Raz, sam seidel, Lenore Skenazy, Barry Svigals, Susie Wise, and Sarah Wolman. Abby vanMuijen and Marc Yu made the design aspects of putting the workbook together a delight. Jess Oh and Beth Eisen were also extraordinarily helpful on the technical end.

As the pandemic wore on, and all the other tumultuous events of the year unfolded, it became clear that things weren't going to happen the way I'd imagined. I increasingly felt like writing this book was something that I needed to do—both for myself and to contribute to the process of healing. So I reached back out to some of the people just mentioned and turned to others who might be able to offer additional perspective. Many thanks to these people as well: Jonathan Blasher, Kevin Carroll, Chris Conard, Charles Cooper, Kyle DeRoos, Tara Doherty, Jo Doyle, Eunice Dunham, Marc Freedman, Jon Gay, Micaela Gerardin-Frey, Odiaka Gonzalez, Richard Johnstin, Amy Jones, JG Larochette, Erin Lewellen, Dana LoVecchio, Paul McAndrew, Hector Salazar, Brian Schmaedick, Michelle Serrano, Pooja Shah, Ralph Smith, Jim Thompson, Mashama Thompson, Joy Weiss, and Adeola Whitney.

I am very grateful to the people whose stories I've told herein—and for all the other stories that contributed to the insights that are reflected. I am also indebted to Playworks staff, Junior Coaches, board members—national and regional—and to our funders. You deserve all the credit for everything that is great about this book, and I take full responsibility for all of the dangling participles and mixed metaphors. I also want to say a special thanks to the Playworks national board members who have been so deeply engaged during the pandemic. You have offered guidance and care when we needed it most, and we are better for it. Throughout this past year, Dick Daniels's leadership as board chair has offered an exemplary balance of calm, care, and a much-needed sense of humor.

On the technical writing side of things, I want to thank Jenn Brown who helped in editing the earliest version, Susan Geraghty for copyediting, Abby vanMuijen for helping me think things through visually, and Eliza Wee for design inspiration. A special note of gratitude to the morning writing accountability group that offered the structure and discipline I needed: Tracey Benson, Ela Ben-Ur, Julia Kramer, and Susie Wise. Tracey, many thanks for taking a look at Big Change 19 as well.

Writing a book also requires an abundance of personal support. On that front, many thanks to Andrea Barnes, Deb Jospin, Simmons Lettre, and John Gomperts. Being a part of Ashoka has been a source of encouragement throughout my career, and this phase has been no exception. I talked to my parents almost every day during this writing process, and they are my archetype for caring, consistent adults. I also happen to really, really like them, which feels lucky. Happily, although slightly strangely, the pandemic meant that most of our adult kids were around way more than anticipated during the writing of this book. It was a bittersweet pleasure to get to spend more time with them, and they have each—in their own way—taught me so much about resilience and love.

Last, but certainly not least, I want to thank Elizabeth Cushing. Elizabeth, you have made all of this possible, from being the person who knew we needed to hotly pursue Robert Wood Johnson funding in 2005 to taking over as CEO when I stepped down, and everything in between. You have led Playworks—both visibly and behind the scenes—and made me better at what I do along the way.

These past couple of years—not just the pandemic, but even before—have asked so much of you, and you have always stepped up. You were the person I turned to when I got stuck in the writing process, and you were there for me, not just as an editor but as a partner. I have said it before, but it bears repeating: you are my "who luck."

Index